change
your
questions
change
your life

MARILEE ADAMS, PhD

change your questions

change your life

12 POWERFUL TOOLS FOR LEADERSHIP, COACHING, AND RESULTS

FOURTH EDITION

Berrett–Koehler Publishers, Inc.

Berrett-Koehler Publishers, Inc.
1333 Broadway, Suite 1000
Oakland, CA 94612-1921
Tel: (510) 817-2277
Fax: (510) 817-2278
www.bkconnection.com

ORDERING INFORMATION

Quantity sales. Special discounts are available on quantity purchases by corporations, associations, and others. For details, contact the "Special Sales Department" at the Berrett-Koehler address above.

Individual sales. Berrett-Koehler publications are available through most bookstores. They can also be ordered directly from Berrett-Koehler: Tel: (800) 929-2929; Fax: (802) 864-7626; www.bkconnection.com.

Orders for college textbook / course adoption use. Please contact Berrett-Koehler: Tel: (800) 929-2929; Fax: (802) 864-7626.

Distributed to the U.S. trade and internationally by Penguin Random House Publisher Services.

Berrett-Koehler and the BK logo are registered trademarks of Berrett-Koehler Publishers, Inc. Chief Question Officer and Q-Storming are registered trademarks of the Inquiry Institute. Question Thinking, Choice Map, Learner Living, and Q-Prep are trademarks of the Inquiry Institute.

Printed in the United States of America

Berrett-Koehler books are printed on long-lasting acid-free paper. When it is available, we choose paper that has been manufactured by environmentally responsible processes. These may include using trees grown in sustainable forests, incorporating recycled paper, minimizing chlorine in bleaching, or recycling the energy produced at the paper mill.

Library of Congress Cataloging-in-Publication Data
Names: Adams, Marilee G., 1945- author.
Title: Change your questions, change your life : 12 powerful tools for
    leadership, coaching, and results / Marilee Adams, PhD.
Description: 4th edition. | Oakland, CA : Berrett-Koehler Publishers,
    [2022] | Includes bibliographical references.
Identifiers: LCCN 2022004275 (print) | LCCN 2022004276 (ebook) | ISBN
    9781523091034 (paperback ; alk. paper) | ISBN 9781523091041 (pdf) | ISBN
    9781523091058 (epub)
Subjects: LCSH: Change (Psychology) | Self-talk.
Classification: LCC BF637.C4 A33 2022 (print) | LCC BF637.C4 (ebook) |
    DDC 158.1—dc23/eng/20220503
LC record available at https://lccn.loc.gov/2022004275
LC ebook record available at https://lccn.loc.gov/2022004276

Fourth Edition

28 27 26 25 24 23 22   10 9 8 7 6 5 4 3 2 1

Book producer: Detta Penna; Text designers: Detta Penna and Lisa Devenish;
Cover designer: Debbie Byrne; Marilee Adams's author photograph by: Tess Steinkolk

For Ed Adams,
my husband and muse

CONTENTS

Foreword by Marshall Goldsmith   ix

Introduction: An Invitation to Question Thinking™   1

1. Moment of Truth   9
2. A Challenge Accepted   17
3. The Choice Map   35
4. We're All Recovering Judgers   51
5. Kitchen Talk   63
6. Switching Questions   73
7. Switching Strategies, Body and Mind   93
8. See with New Eyes, Hear with New Ears   109
9. Learner Teams and Judger Teams   117
10. When the Magic Works   129
11. Q-Storming® to the Rescue   143
12. *Amour! Amour!*   155
13. Coming Full Circle   163
14. The Inquiring Leader   175
QT Tools: The Users Guide   181

Discussion Guide   211
Notes   215
Glossary   217
Acknowledgments   219
About the Author   221
About Inquiry Institute   223

Figures

1. The Choice Map 36–37
2. Learner/Judger Questions 48
3. The Switching Lane 75
4. Learner/Judger Mindset Chart 86
5. Learner/Judger Relationship Chart 87
6. ABCD Choice Process 111

FOREWORD

Marshall Goldsmith, PhD

Very few books ever get popular enough to merit a fourth edition. I'm not at all surprised that *Change Your Questions, Change Your Life* has reached those rarified heights! You might wonder how reading Marilee Adams' invaluable book can help you and the people who are important to you have better lives—in business and personally. This is the key question I urge you to keep in mind as you read the practical wisdom in these pages. The great ideas presented here, in a system of tools Marilee calls Question Thinking, provide a solid new way of thinking that can make a positive difference in all our personal lives and with our teams and organizations.

There are many ideas in this book that helped me. You're sure to find some that will help you, too. *Change Your Questions, Change Your Life* provides methods, skills, and tools for easily implementing Question Thinking, both at work and at home. To start, Marilee shows how we can become more effective and efficient by focusing on learning rather than being judgmental. As a Buddhist, I know this approach is key to having a happier, more productive life.

Marilee shows us the power of questions to direct our thinking and therefore our actions and results. This means that we can intentionally affect the future by designing the most powerful questions for getting us there. That's what great coaching is all about. It's also what great leaders do—they provide us with visions of new futures. Marilee offers Question Thinking Tools for both coaches and leaders to optimize and fulfill their missions.

It was predictable that *Change Your Questions, Change Your Life* would become an international bestseller. It's made so much of a real difference in people's lives that they've shared the book with their colleagues, teams, and companies and also with their families and friends. One of the stories in the Introduction says it all—a reader wrote Marilee that he used the methods in the book so successfully that his company got a mention in Inc. Magazine. That kind of success is why so many coaches use the Question Thinking methods and also give the book to their clients.

In my mission as an executive coach, I help successful leaders get better with measurable results. This includes teaching a process called feed forward. Leaders learn to ask for ideas to move the future. They refine their ability to listen without judgment and to say "thank you" for suggestions. Marilee would call this "listening with Learner ears," which is invaluable for all coaches, leaders, and managers. It's also the basis for her seminal concept of inquiring leadership.

Racecar drivers are taught to "focus on the road—not the wall." As you read this book, focus on the road that represents your highest potential by asking questions that lead to a better future, such as: "What are the greatest positive possibilities I can imagine?"

The fourth edition delivers even more than the first three, incorporating important new material. *Change Your Questions, Change Your Life* has great wisdom for us all. Take it very seriously. Roll up your sleeves and get to work. A Buddhist text advises that just reading about a medicine won't bring healing; one actually has to take the medicine. So, my advice is that the best way to get the most out of this book is to practice everything in it!

Life is good!

Dr. Marshall Goldsmith is the only two-time Thinkers 50: #1 Leadership Thinker in the World and has been a Top Ten Business Thinker for eight consecutive years. He is a #1 *New York Times* bestselling author of *What Got You Here Won't Get You There*, *Triggers*, and *The Earned Life*.

An Invitation to Question Thinking

One summer afternoon, shortly after the first edition of this book was published, I answered my office phone to hear a man's booming voice announce, "You don't know me, but I'm Ben." He laughed, and I laughed along with him because I knew exactly what he was referring to. Ben, the main character in this book, is a composite I created, based on real life clients I have coached over the past thirty years. This caller had identified with Ben's situation so thoroughly that he was convinced I could also help him and his organization get the results they needed.

Ben has become almost legendary for many of my readers. In the story—a business fable through which readers experience the practical power of Question Thinking (QT)—Ben is floundering in his new leadership position. He's also having trouble at home. His relationship with Grace, his wife of less than a year, is growing increasingly tense. When we first meet him, Ben is one unhappy guy. With the help of his coach and mentor, Joseph S. Edwards, he not only advances in his professional life but also deepens his bond with his wife.

Since that first telephone call from a "Ben," I've received many similar messages from both men and women from a wide variety of backgrounds. One reader, David, wrote that like Ben, he'd been in trouble at work, especially with keeping his team fully engaged. Reading the book not only changed the questions he asked himself, but his new leadership style encouraged greater collaboration and productivity. He was ultimately so successful that his results were included in an article in *Inc.* magazine. You'll find that article and other references in the notes at the end of this book.

The world has changed dramatically since the last edition of *Change Your Questions,* making Question Thinking skills more crucial than ever for dealing with the rising social, economic, health, and environmental challenges confronting us. Through the internet and other digital media, we are bombarded by wide-ranging opinions and widely varying sources of information. Without an ability to question and critically evaluate what we take in, the cumulative impact of these experiences fuels our anxiety, uncertainty, discord, and effectiveness as leaders and as human beings. QT skills support our ability to navigate these rough waters with resilience, adaptability, thoughtfulness, and hope.

Question Thinking, the heart of this book, provides easy-to-learn skills for observing and evaluating our present thinking—especially the questions we're asking ourselves—and guides us in designing new questions for achieving more fulfilling experiences and results. QT is about thinking mindfully rather than reactively.

It leads to more productive outcomes, even under pressure, while building reliable capacities for constructive thought, so vital for sustainable change in our professional as well as personal lives. Without these skills, even our greatest aspirations may remain only wishes and dreams.

Question Thinking began with an important moment of discovery in my own life. I was a determined young graduate student working away on my PhD dissertation. Not only did I endure a ruthless inner critic, but criticisms from others often left me in tears. One fateful day, expecting high praise from my advisor for some work I felt great about, I instead heard him say: "Marilee, this is just not acceptable." At that moment something new happened. I started going to that old place of tearfully wondering what was wrong with me. But then, I began observing myself, and watching not only what I was thinking but how I was thinking. I observed that all the negativity that made me so unhappy was in the form of questions I was asking myself. They were questions like: "What's wrong with me? Why can't I ever get anything right? What makes me think I have anything to offer? How come everybody else is so much smarter and more successful than me?"

Anyone who's spent much time trying to answer questions like these will recognize how stuck and frustrating this can be. This time, instead of getting caught up in these questions, I paused and took a deep breath. Becoming calm and curious, I simply asked myself, "Okay, how do I fix it?" That simple switch in my thinking took me from feeling powerless to being confident enough to take constructive action. I was able to give my inner critic a rest and calmly consider my advisor's suggestions. Soon I was rewriting the section he had found unacceptable, and to my surprise I came up with new possibilities that greatly improved my work.

Of course, I had to wonder, "What had happened?! What made such a difference this time?" I realized that my old familiar judgmental questions about what was wrong and not good enough about me seemed to have evaporated. Rather than getting stuck in that awful quagmire of self-criticism and self-doubt, I had instead focused on the future with the goal of having my questions work for me rather than against me.

Was that change of mine just a fluke? Was there a way to turn this seeming miracle into a reliable method for intentional change for myself and others? From such modest beginnings blossomed this body of work that today I call Question Thinking—which points to how we think with questions and how these questions affect our life experiences and outcomes. In their book, *Coaching with the Brain in Mind: Foundations for Practice,* coauthors David Rock and Linda J. Page described one of the core benefits of my work: "People typically are not aware of their internal questions or of the profound power they exert in shaping and directing their experiences and lives. By changing those questions, one can set in motion a different process leading to a different result."

If you are a coach or any kind of change agent—team leader, department head, or CEO—the QT methodology can become an integral part of each conversation, providing intuitive skills for self-coaching, greater self-awareness, and improved effectiveness in whatever you do.

It's always deeply satisfying to have readers and clients share their success stories with me. One such story, involving a company called Flextronics, was reported in the Wharton@Work Newsletter, which I reference in the notes at the back of the book. Flextronics—renamed Flex—is a global leader in electronics manufacturing and distribution in about 30 countries. Using the principles of Question Thinking, Carmella, the Senior Director of Organizational Effectiveness, coached to success the leaders of what had been a poorly performing operations site. This was no mean feat since it involved about 700 people in a site that had had the lowest scores of the 15 in their division.

Carmella assigned the site leaders to read *Change Your Questions* and share the book with their teams. She then coached the leaders in the use of a tool I call Q-Storming—brain-storming on steroids—ultimately solving what had been daunting and costly problems. (I describe the use of this tool in Chapter 11.) Within three months, Carmella's QT based coaching was credited with the site's dramatic turnaround. They moved to the #1 spot in their division and maintained a position among the top sites year after year.

A different kind of story touched me in another way. Jason, a workshop participant, talked about coming home to find his wife Pam in a panic in his basement office. Water poured down from a flood in the kitchen above, threatening his computer and media equipment. Jason told us, "The old me would have snapped into blame mode." Instead, his Question Thinking skills kicked in. He took a deep breath and told himself, "This is not about blame." Instead, he asked himself, "What do I need to do right away? How do we stop the flood?" He quickly shut off the water and called the plumber. In his soggy downstairs office, Pam sobbed, "This was your whole world, Jason. And I nearly ruined it." Jason said that thanks to learning Question Thinking, he had the presence of mind to reply, "No, Sweetheart, you're my whole world." He later told me, "At that moment I knew it was time to let go of what I'd collected and never let anything ruin what was really important in my life."

These stories illustrate the universal applicability of Question Thinking. At work it's useful regardless of your role or where you are in your career; that's why it's so widely used in businesses and organizations. As a benefit in our personal lives, readers gain new tools and skills to make their lives and relationships happier and more fulfilled.

When, with well over 400,000 copies sold, my publisher asked me to write a fourth edition of this book, I took the opportunity to expand on what I'd learned over the years from my clients, students, and workshop participants. Their contributions have been invaluable and have often helped me to see new applications of QT. Notably, for 10 years my wonderful students in the Key Executive Leadership Program at American University taught me much that has expanded my thinking about Inquiring Leadership. I've woven what my clients and students taught me into the book in the form of stories and anecdotes, and used these insights to enhance the practical application of the QT tools you'll find near the back of the book.

Because so many people and organizations requested it, I've added a book Discussion Guide, describing ways to have the most meaningful conversations about the concepts and tools in this book. You'll also find a glossary for quickly clarifying the main terms in the book.

I'm especially excited about integrating some of the fascinating discoveries in the burgeoning world of neuroscience. There's a whole new chapter in the story about what brain scientists have discovered about our responses to everyday challenges, fostering a new appreciation for the brain's ability to constantly expand its abilities. These discoveries help us understand how Question Thinking can profoundly impact what we are able to achieve in personal progress as well as with team and leadership development. Gaining a sense of what the neurosciences can teach us about mindsets not only helps to demystify the process of change, but it can also provide us with confidence in the possibility and "how to" of change, building resilience and positive habits.

In *The Art of the Question,* my first book, I wrote that "with our questions we make the world." Questions open our minds, our eyes, and our hearts. With our questions we learn, connect, and create. We are smarter, more productive, and able to get better results. We shift our orientation from fixed opinions and easy answers to curiosity, thoughtful questions, and open-minded conversations, lighting the way to collaboration, deeper connections, discovery, and innovation. I have a vision of workplaces and a society—of individuals, families, organizations, and communities—that are vibrant with this spirit of inquiry and possibility.

If the power of self-coaching appeals to you, check out the *Change Your Questions, Change Your Life Workbook: Master Your Mindset Using Question Thinking.*

Now it's time to meet Ben—the fictional character I've created to represent my ideas in this book. You're about to discover, in Ben's own words, how changing your questions really can change your life.

CHAPTER 1

Moment of Truth

"If we would have new knowledge, we must
get us a whole world of new questions."

Susanne K. Langer

A rosewood paperweight on my desk bears a sterling silver plaque declaring: Great results begin with great questions. It was a gift from a very special person in my life—Joseph S. Edwards—who introduced me to Question Thinking, or QT, as he called the skills he taught me. QT opened a part of my mind that otherwise I might never have discovered. Like everyone else, I believed the way to fix a problem was to look for the right answers. Instead, Joseph showed me that the best way to solve a problem is to first come up with better questions. The skills he taught me rescued my career and saved my marriage as well. Both were definitely in trouble at the time.

It all started when I was invited to take a leadership position at QTec. The company was amidst a major overhaul at the time, and the word on the street was that, barring a miracle, they would fold before the year was out. A friend warned me that accepting a position with QTec would be like signing up to crew on a sinking ship. What convinced me to take the risk? It was my trust in Alexa

Harte, the recently appointed CEO at QTec, who'd offered me the position. I'd worked with her for years at KBCorp, my previous employer, where she'd won my respect as a gifted leader. Her confidence about turning QTec around was infectious. Besides, she promised me a great promotion: hefty pay raise, impressive title, and a chance to lead a team in developing an innovative new product. If everything went well the risk would pay off in aces. If not... well, I tried not to think about that.

At first, I was riding high, convinced I had the job wired. Part of me really loved the idea of leading the group and working with my team. But there was more to the picture. Alexa had hired me for my technology and engineering smarts, and I knew I could deliver in that regard. The new product really intrigued me, and the technological challenges were right up my alley. At KB— where Alexa said she'd seen me work miracles—I'd won accolades as the Answer Man. I'd faced down the toughest technical problems, one right after the other. However, at QTec I was facing a different kind of challenge—leading a high-stakes, high-visibility team. I was excited about taking this on, although Alexa had let me know I'd have to put effort into developing my people and leadership skills.

My team seemed an enthusiastic and talented bunch, and I'd been excited about taking over the reins of the project. For a while, everything went well. In fact, very well. Then life at QTec started unraveling. It was as if suddenly a glaring spotlight was focused on my shortcomings. I didn't dare say it, but secretly I concluded I'd been stuck with a bunch of losers.

To make matters worse, there was Charles. Before I came

aboard at QTec he'd been passed over for the job I'd been offered. I could understand why he might resent me. And, just as I expected, he was a real troublemaker from the word go, questioning everything I said and did.

Things went from bad to worse. If the QTec ship wasn't actually sinking, as my friend had warned me, it was definitely taking on water. As captain of that ship I had no idea how to plug up the leaks. My team meetings became a farce—no discussions, no solutions, and no sense of teamwork. And nobody had to remind me that if we couldn't get our product to market before the competition, we would prove the naysayers right.

Life wasn't much better at home. Tension was growing with Grace, my wonderful wife of less than eight months. She constantly asked me about what was going on at work. Finally, one day I just told her she was asking too many questions and she should keep her nose out of my business. She was hurt, I was miserable, and I hadn't the vaguest idea what to do about it.

I didn't want Grace to know how much difficulty I was having. I'd always taken great pride in solving problems that baffled everyone else. This time, with any luck, the right answers would turn up before Grace, Alexa, and the people on my team found out that the job was way over my head. Meanwhile I kept more and more to myself and did my best to just get through each day.

I was mystified and overwhelmed. It seemed like everything in my life was falling apart. Then came the awful turning point. Grace and I had an argument in the morning, and only hours later there was a major crisis at work. Nobody said it, but I could see it in their eyes: we were cooked.

This was my moment of truth. I needed to be alone and face facts. I called Grace and left a message that I'd be putting in an all-nighter to finish an important report. Then I spent the whole long night in my office, staring at the walls, still searching desperately for the right answers, and reliving the most disastrous weeks of my life. I told myself I had to face the truth: I had failed. Just after six that morning I went out for coffee and then started drafting my resignation. I finished three hours later, called Alexa, and arranged to see her immediately.

The walk to Alexa's suite was less than a hundred yards. That morning it felt like a hundred miles. When I got to the big double doors of her office I stopped and took a deep breath to regain my composure. I stood there for some long moments, working up the nerve to knock. Just as I was raising my arm, I heard a voice behind me.

"Ben Knight, you're here. Good, good!"

It was Alexa. There was no mistaking that voice, always cheerful, exuding a sense of optimism even when things were going badly. An attractive, athletic-looking woman in her late 40s, she radiated confidence. I'd told Grace that I'd never met anyone quite like Alexa. She approached her responsibilities at QTec with boundless enthusiasm. It wasn't that she didn't take her job seriously. She took it very seriously! And she did it with such pleasure and self-assurance that she made it look easy.

At that moment, her mere presence made me acutely aware of my deficiencies. I felt numb, barely mumbling a subdued good morning as she touched my shoulder and ushered me into her office.

The room was expansive, the size of a large living room in the best executive home. I crossed deep green carpeting, soft underfoot, and walked over to the large bay window where the meeting area was set up. There, two overstuffed sofas faced each other across a large walnut coffee table.

"Sit!" Alexa said, gesturing in a welcoming way to one of the couches. "Betty said your lights were on when she left her office at seven-thirty last night, and you were here when she came in early this morning."

She sat down across from me on the other couch.

"I presume that's for me?" Alexa asked, pointing to the green folder containing my resignation that I'd placed on the coffee table.

I nodded, waiting for her to pick it up. Instead, she leaned back, looking as if she had all the time in the world.

"Tell me what's going on with you," she said.

I pointed to the green folder. "It's my resignation. I'm sorry, Alexa."

The next sound I heard stopped me cold. It was not a gasp, not a word of reproach, but laughter! It was not cruel laughter, either. What had I missed? I didn't understand. How could Alexa still sound sympathetic in the face of all I'd screwed up?

"Ben," she said, "you're not going to quit on me." She slid the folder in my direction. "Take this back. I know more about your situation than you realize. I want you to give me at least a few months. But during that time you've got to commit to making changes."

"Are you sure about this?" I asked, dumbfounded.

"Let me answer you this way," she continued. "Many years

ago, I was in a situation similar to yours. I had to face facts. If I wanted to be successful, I'd need to make some fundamental changes. I was desperate. A man by the name of Joseph sat me down and asked some straightforward questions that seemed simple on the surface. But those questions opened doors I never even knew existed. He asked, 'Are you willing to take responsibility for your mistakes— and for the attitudes, mindsets and actions that led to them?' Then he said, 'Are you willing—however begrudgingly—to forgive yourself, and even laugh at yourself?' And finally, 'Will you look for value in your experiences, especially the most difficult ones?' Bottom line: 'Are you willing to learn from what happened and make changes accordingly?'"

She went on to tell me how Joseph's work with her, and the methods he had developed over the years, had changed not only her life but her husband Stan's as well. Stan has more than tripled his net worth in the past few years. He attributes the success he and his company enjoy today to what Joseph taught him. Joseph will probably tell you all about it. He loves to tell stories, especially ones about how people's lives were changed by changing their questions."

I must have looked perplexed because she added, "Don't worry about what I mean by questions that change people's lives. You'll learn about that soon enough." She paused. Then, in carefully measured words, she said, "I want you to work with my friend Joseph, starting immediately. I'm sure he'll want to meet with you over a period of time. Figure out the schedule with him. This is top priority now."

"What is he, a therapist?" The idea of seeing a shrink made me nervous.

Alexa smiled. "No, he's an executive coach. I call him an inquiring coach."

Inquiring coach! If I knew anything at all, it was that I needed answers, not more questions. How could more questions possibly benefit me or pull me out of the hole I was in?

As I was getting ready to leave, Alexa jotted something down on a piece of paper and sealed it in an envelope. "Inside this envelope is a prediction I've made," she said mysteriously, handing it to me. "Put it in that green folder of yours and don't open it until you've completed your work with Joseph and I tell you it's the time to open it." Then she gave me Joseph's business card. I turned it over. There was a big question mark on the other side. It really irritated me. The idea that I'd be spending valuable time with a man whose logo was a question mark went against everything I believed.

Back in my own office, I collapsed in the chair behind my desk. My eyes fell on a small, gilded frame on the wall. It held a saying, just two words long: Question everything! It was a quote attributed to Albert Einstein. Many rooms at QTec contained a framed placard exactly like this one. As much as I respected and appreciated Alexa's leadership, this message had always been a point of contention for me. Everybody knows that leaders should have answers, not questions.

"Question everything!"
Albert Einstein

My eyes were fixed on Joseph's card with the question mark on the back. What had I gotten myself into? Only time would tell. At least I could put off my decision to resign. My attention shifted to Grace. How was I ever going to smooth things over with her? At that moment there was only one thing to be grateful for—Alexa hadn't asked about Grace and me. I think that would have been the last straw. I knew Alexa was fond of my wife—she'd even come to our wedding. She wouldn't have been happy to find out we were having trouble.

I sat there for a long time just staring at Joseph's card. The fact that Alexa had refused to accept my resignation offered a little hope. I was encouraged that she would refer me to her own mentor—even though the jury was still out on whether her trust in me was justified. Still, I had nothing to lose by keeping an appointment with this inquiring coach guy. Besides, even though I was skeptical, I was also curious. If Joseph had helped Alexa and Stan so much, maybe he had answers that would help me, too.

CHAPTER 2

A Challenge Accepted

"What got you here won't get you there."

Marshall Goldsmith

My appointment with Joseph S. Edwards was at ten the next morning. I hadn't told Grace about this meeting or about my conversation with Alexa. And I certainly didn't tell her about writing my resignation. Admitting I was in trouble had never come easily for me. I preferred working things out on my own. For some time now I'd been stonewalling Grace and feeling more and more impatient with her questions about what was going on with me. I told myself she had her own problems. At the non-profit where she worked, the push was on to update and resubmit two important grants. Added to this, her assistant, Jennifer, a new volunteer, wasn't turning out to be the self-starter Grace had expected. She didn't need to be worrying about me. Until I found the right answers and solutions, I was determined to tough it out and keep my problems to myself. But as usually happened with Grace, I wasn't so good at hiding my problems.

I should have realized that she knew something more than the usual job stress was bothering me. That morning, on our way to the airport, where Grace was catching a plane for a lunch meeting in another city, she brought things to a head. As I pulled up to the curb at the terminal, she told me, "I've been feeling like a widow lately. You've been so distant and moody. Ben, if you want a real partnership with me, you're going to have to make some changes."

God knows I love Grace, but I wasn't in the best of moods.

"I don't need this right now," I told her, more harshly than I intended.

Grace looked stunned. I got out of the car to get her briefcase from the trunk. As I handed it to her our eyes met, and for a moment I was afraid she was going to cry. I knew it wasn't right leaving her like that, but I was feeling pushed. Besides, if I got dragged into a long discussion, I'd be late for my appointment with Joseph. Our little problem would have to wait. Grace forced a smile and told me she'd be back that night but not to worry about picking her up. She'd get a taxi home. She turned and quickly disappeared into the crowd.

I was angry. Why did she have to choose this particular morning to pick a fight? I hit the accelerator and pulled out into traffic. Horns blasted. I slammed on my brakes as some maniac raced by, barely missing me. I was fuming. Between that near collision, the conflict with Grace, and having to attend a meeting I dreaded, my morning was off to a very bad start.

Joseph's office was in the Pearl Building downtown, a 14-story edifice constructed in the 1930s and recently restored. Old Town, as we called the area, was a bustling shopping center with great places to eat and drink, and unusual little stores. Grace and I often had dinner there, at a small place called the Metropol. Grace is an art lover, and she'd opened up a whole new world I'd hardly known existed. Thanks to her, we'd spent many happy hours together browsing through bookstores and art galleries. Passing our familiar haunts that morning, I worried about what the future held for us.

I pushed open the polished brass-framed doors at the Pearl Building, crossed the marble floors, and caught an elevator to Joseph's penthouse office. I stepped into a large foyer that looked like someone's private residence. Several tall Ficus trees reached up toward a large skylight.

Beyond this private anteroom, a double set of doors opened invitingly to a long hallway. On the walls hung some kind of artwork. I remember thinking that Grace would enjoy seeing this.

"You must be Ben Knight!" Joseph Edwards strode toward me enthusiastically. I judged him to be in his early 60s, though he moved like an agile sprinter a quarter that age. No more than 5 feet 9, he was dressed casually, wearing an outrageous knit sweater with a myriad of striped patterns that dazzled the eye. He was not at all like I'd expected.

Joseph's smooth-shaven face glowed with good humor. His brown eyes sparkled with almost childlike excitement. Atop his head, a wild array of woolly white curls reminded me of photos I'd seen of Albert Einstein in his later years.

Joseph's warm welcome dissolved some of my reservations about spending time with him. He led me down the hallway to his office, explaining as we went that the walls displayed "some artifacts I call my Question Thinking Hall of Fame." What I had at first mistaken for artworks were actually framed magazine articles and letters. We turned left into a large room bathed in the morning sunlight.

The room contained comfortable seating, a well-used brick fireplace, and a walnut conference table with matching chairs. One wall displayed certificates and a few dozen autographed photos, many with their subjects shaking hands with Joseph. In the pictures I recognized faces I'd seen in the news over the years. Alexa hadn't quite prepared me for this. Joseph was obviously very well connected in the business world and beyond.

I also saw covers of three different books displayed in elegant frames. They were all written by Joseph. Each had the words Question Thinking in the title. One in particular caught my eye. It was co-authored with a Sarah Edwards and was about inquiring marriages.

I was impressed but also intimidated. We entered a less formal room, where I felt slightly more comfortable. Windows on three sides afforded a spectacular view of the city. In the distance, wispy clouds were lifting from the woods. The views seemed to stretch on forever.

I eased myself into a large leather armchair while Joseph took his place near me in a matching one. He dangled a pair of rimless reading glasses from his left hand.

After some brief get-acquainted conversation, he asked, "Tell me, what do you suppose is your greatest asset?"

"I'm the Answer Man, the Go-To guy," I told him with pride. "I've built my whole career around being the person people go to for answers. The bottom line for me is answers and results. That's what business is all about."

"True. But how can you get the best answers without first asking the best questions?" Joseph paused, placing his glasses on his

> How can you get the best answers without first
> asking the best questions?

nose and peering over the top of them at me: "Is there a single question you would say characterizes the way you operate?"

"Sure," I said. "Get the right answers and be ready to back them up, that's my motto."

Joseph asked me to restate that as a question, one I would ask myself. I couldn't see the point, but I did as he asked, "Okay. Sure. The question I operate with is, How can I prove I'm right?

"That's great," Joseph said. "Then we might have your problem nailed already."

"My problem?"

"Being the answer man. Having to prove you're right," Joseph said. "I must say, Ben, we're getting down to business faster than I expected."

I wasn't sure if I'd heard him correctly. Was he kidding? No, he was dead serious. "I beg your pardon?"

"Finding proof that our answers are correct can be important," he said. "But would you allow that there are times when too much of a good thing can get you in trouble? For example, how do you think your having to be right all the time goes over with your team?"

"I'm not sure what you mean," I said, and I really meant it. I wanted my team to find answers, the correct answers. "Everyone's looking for answers." That's what we all get paid to do, isn't it?

"Let me get personal for a moment," Joseph said. "Do your efforts to prove you're right work with your wife?"

That one hit home. "Not really," I admitted. Grace had told me how my habit of insisting on being right often frustrated her.

"It doesn't work so well with my wife either," Joseph said smiling. "With that in mind, let's look a little deeper into what questions really do. Certainly we recognize that questions are a vital part of communication. But the role they play in thinking is not always obvious, and that's where Question Thinking skills can be invaluable.

"If you're willing to grab onto the real power of questions, they can change your whole life. It comes down to increasing the quantity and quality of the questions we ask ourselves and others. It also matters enormously what our intentions are when we ask those questions. As the Romanian playwright Eugène Ionesco famously said, 'It is not the answer that enlightens, but the question.'"

I must have looked puzzled, because Joseph paused and said, "You've never heard the term Question Thinking before, have you?"

I shook my head, no.

"Question Thinking is a system of skills and tools using questions to expand how you approach virtually any situation. It's about developing skills to refine your questions for vastly better results in anything you do. That begins with asking questions of ourselves, and only then asking them of others. The QT system, that is, Question Thinking, can literally put action into your thinking—action that's focused, creative, and effective. It's a great way to create a foundation for making wiser choices."

> Question Thinking is a system of tools
> for transforming thinking, action, and
> results through skillful question asking
> —questions we ask ourselves
> as well as those we ask others.

"Go on," I said, skeptically.

"Much of the time we're barely conscious of asking questions, especially the ones we ask ourselves. But questions are a part of our thought process nearly every moment of our lives. Thinking actually occurs as an internal question-and-answer process. Not only that, we often answer our own questions by taking some action, by doing something.

"Here's an example. When you got dressed this morning, I'll bet you went to your closet, or dresser—or maybe even the floor—and asked yourself questions like: Where am I going? What's the weather? What's comfortable? Or even, What's clean? You answered your questions by making a quick decision and then doing something. You selected some clothing and put it on. You are, in effect, wearing your answers."

"I guess I can't argue with that. As you say, though, if I did ask those questions, I hardly noticed it at the time. Actually, my biggest question was whether Grace picked up my clothes at the cleaners, like she promised."

We both laughed.

Joseph was on a roll. It seemed like a good idea to just sit back and hear him out. Besides, I was getting intrigued.

"When we get stuck," Joseph continued, "it's natural to go on a hunt for answers and solutions. But in doing so we often unintentionally put up blocks instead of creating openings. I always remember that wonderful quote of Albert Einstein's: 'We cannot solve our problems with the same thinking we used when we created them.' To solve our problems, we first need to change our questions. Otherwise we'll probably just keep getting the same old answers, over and over again.

"We cannot solve our problems with the same thinking we used when we created them."

Albert Einstein

"New questions can totally shift our perspectives, moving us into fresh ways of looking at problems. The questions we ask can even change the course of history, sometimes dramatically. Let me give you an example. Long ago, nomadic societies were driven by the implicit question How do we get ourselves to water?"

I nodded. "Which is what kept them nomadic…"

"Yet look what happened when their implicit question changed to How do we get water to come to us? That new question initiated one of humanity's most significant paradigm shifts. It ushered in agriculture, including the invention of irrigation, the storage of water, digging wells, and eventually the creation of cities, often many miles from water. Just think of Las Vegas. That new question changed peoples' behavior, changed the course of history, and we can never go back."

"I guess I can see how questions apply to getting dressed and even to that paradigm shift for nomads. But how does this apply to business? And more to the point, how can it help me with my problems?"

"The point is that questions drive results," Joseph responded. "They virtually program how we think, the actions we take and what kinds of outcomes are possible. Consider three companies, each one driven by one of the following questions: What's the best way to satisfy shareholders? What's the best way to satisfy customers? What's the best way to satisfy employees? In terms of a business, each question will point the organization in a different direction, influencing, if not dictating its strategies for achieving its goals. Remember: Questions drive results. That's as true in your day-to-day life at QTec as it was for nomads thousands of years ago.

Questions drive results.

"Your ideas are interesting," I hedged. "But I've literally built my reputation on having answers...not questions."

"Fortunately," Joseph continued, "the route from being an answer man to becoming a question man is much shorter than you might think."

What was he suggesting? Giving up my cherished role as the answer man was about the furthest thing from my mind. I wasn't about to give up something that had worked so well for me for so long. One thing I was pretty certain of—if we'd stuck with only questions, we'd still be scratching our heads and hunting for our suppers with pointed sticks. Joseph removed his glasses and paused, as if contemplating what he was going to say next. Then he spoke in a slow, even voice.

"Ben, you've got to face facts here—you're in trouble. One of your greatest assets—being the answer man—has turned into a liability. That's the bottom line."

As Joseph spoke, I imagined Grace sitting here in his office with me. Truly, she would applaud what he was saying. A big knot tightened in my belly.

"If being the answer man was still working for you," Joseph continued, "you wouldn't have spent the night in your office writing your resignation. Alexa told me about that. I know where you were coming from. I've had my own share of all-night debates with the walls of my office.

"This is where I think I can help you," he said. "Alexa has been watching your career for a long time. She believes you've got great potential, and she's obviously invested a lot in you. But she also thinks that without some big changes you won't make it as a leader at QTec. She knows you pretty well, Ben. Before she hired you, she shared her concerns with me about bringing you into the company. She especially had questions about your readiness for a leadership position. If I'm not mistaken, she also told you what she was worried about. Alexa is not exactly a shrinking violet."

We both laughed at that comment, and I was grateful for a moment of levity. Alexa was about the most forthright human being I'd ever met. She never beat around the bush.

With more than a little embarrassment, I remembered her exact words the day she hired me: "Ben, I'm bringing you in because you're absolutely the best in your field. I'm completely confident about your technical acumen, which we need for the new markets we plan to open up. What I'm not as comfortable with is your people skills. That's where you need to improve if you're going to make it as a leader. I'm gambling on you and I'm planning on winning this bet."

At the time, I had brushed off Alexa's warning. Instead, I had immediately called Grace to tell her about my great coup. If I'd heard Alexa's warning at all, it was filtered through the plans I was making for a victory celebration with my wife that evening.

"As an answer man," Joseph said, "your dogged determination to find the right answers has led you to some brilliant breakthroughs. However, the line between having the right answers and being perceived as a know-it-all can indeed be thin. You could even come off as arrogant and uncaring. My guess is that with the added pressure and responsibility of your new position, that know-it-all style has gotten exaggerated. Once you get labeled, you're in trouble. When others start seeing you that way, can you really expect them to like or respect or trust you? It's not exactly an ideal leadership profile."

"Who's running a popularity contest here?" I countered. In my mind, a good leader has one responsibility—get the job done and see that others follow through on their assignments. Nobody on my team was producing.

"Whenever you're interacting with other people as a leader," Joseph said, "you want them to take initiative, be resilient, ask questions, and come up with better solutions, ones that maybe you hadn't thought of yourself. Your accomplishments come from the collective efforts of the people you're working with, not just from your own solitary work. The skills that allowed you to create such dazzling technological breakthroughs in the past are not the same skills you need to be successful as a leader. In the words of Marshall Goldsmith, 'What got you here won't get you there.'"

Joseph went to his desk and took a binder with a printed cover from the side drawer. As he handed it to me, I read the title: QT Tools: The Users Guide to Question Thinking. I began flipping through the pages.

"If it's true that you're coming across as a know-it-all," he continued, "which is the downfall of the Answer Man, you don't leave much room for anyone else. You're great at the technical stuff, Ben, but your present job requires much more than that. You're working with people, not objects. Where people are concerned, there's a certain magic in getting just the right mixture between questions and answers. I can offer this suggestion: Start by asking more and telling a lot less. The most effective communication is much more about asking and much less about telling. Unless you do ask questions, how can you make room for new information or find out what people are thinking or needing? Conventional wisdom has it upside down—in fact, even most formal communication courses usually focus on telling and not nearly enough on the importance of asking questions.

> Ask more. Tell less. Get curious. And not just about technical issues. Ask, What can I do to get people more engaged? What can I do to get people working collaboratively? What do others need from me? What do they have to contribute that I haven't been noticing?

"Seems to me you're putting way too much emphasis on questions," I said. "Everyone has questions. That's a no-brainer. But in my experience, it's the guy with answers who makes things happen."

"Face it, Ben, you've hit a wall. Are you going to climb over it? Alexa is convinced you will. It's your choice, not mine, so I can't answer that question for you. Here are some more questions you might ask yourself: Do I really listen to people's questions and suggestions? Do other people in my life feel that I listen to their questions and suggestions? Do they see me as a person that respects and trusts them? Do they feel I am inviting them to take risks and share their ideas?"

Joseph paused. "You look perplexed," he said. "Want to share what's going on with you?"

It took me a moment to collect my thoughts. The truth is, I hadn't expected this meeting to get so personal. When I asked myself those questions about my interactions with other people, I was taken aback, though I still didn't get the point. "All this theory might be fine," I finally managed to say, "but these soft skills just seem, well, soft. I thought we'd be discussing something really practical, something to get actual results, to turn things around."

Joseph laughed in a friendly way. "Don't underestimate soft skills. We ignore them at our peril." "That sounds like Alexa," I said.

Joseph nodded. "Yes, those are her words exactly. She also says, 'In today's world it's not enough to have top technical expertise.' Soft skills, as I refer to them here, refer to skills for communicating more effectively and constructively. That goes a long way toward creating a place where people like to work, and where they give their best. In addition, they are skills for optimizing our own mental abilities, and for expanding our emotional intelligence. Think of these so-called soft skills, these people skills, as the cornerstones of leadership success. You can take that to the bank. The good news is that these skills are learnable…and teachable."

"You and I have very different ways of thinking," I said. "You think in questions. I think in answers. You're going to have to prove to me that this Question Thinking stuff can be practical enough to make a difference with my problems."

"Fair enough," Joseph said. "Let's start with another question: Would you agree that you're looking for ways to change?"

I shrugged. "Isn't the fact that I'm here proof enough that I'm looking for changes?" Truthfully, I was thinking what kind of nonsense is he promoting here? But I didn't say it. I didn't say anything.

"To change something, you need to first understand where you're starting from. The better you can observe that, the more effective you'll be with making the changes you want. And that's where Question Thinking can help you. Really effective, intentional change begins with strengthening your observer self. The better you can see what's going on—that's where the observer self comes in—the better you can apply the right skills and strategies to make the changes you want."

Joseph's emphasis on the observer self piqued my interest. I was familiar with using this observer part of myself to solve technical problems by looking at what was working, what wasn't working, and coming up with answers to solve a problem. But I had never looked through that observer lens when it came to how I interact with other people. The truth is, I'd hardly given much thought to developing people skills or....what was it he called it? Emotional intelligence. Nor had I thought of people skills as something that could be taught the way Joseph was doing it.

"The first tool listed in The Users Guide to Question Thinking is for honing your skills as an observer," Joseph said. "Before we meet next time, read it over. I suspect you'll find ways you're already applying these skills."

I nodded absently as I scanned the tool he was talking about. Ready or not, the self-observing questions were already coming. First and foremost was, "Should I be questioning my assumption about the power of answers?" I was beginning to suspect I might be missing something if I didn't pay attention to Joseph. The notion that Grace might agree with him was also playing at the back of my mind. Was I doing too much telling and not enough asking with my wife? I suspect I already knew the answer to that question.

"Judging by the look on your face, I'm guessing you're a little unsettled right now," Joseph said. "But I assure you that once you understand how to use the Question Thinking principles and practices, particularly in strengthening your ability to observe yourself, all the pieces will fall into place. Think of the tools I've described as guidance into this world of questions. I promise that these tools provide a practical how-to that makes real change possible. You have no idea what a powerful difference this can make for your career." Joseph flashed me an enigmatic smile and added, "To say nothing of what it can do for your personal relationships."

I've got to admit, Joseph's remark about my personal relationships pushed my buttons. There was a part of me that wanted to cover my ears and hum the national anthem like we did as kids. But as much as I wanted to protest, I had to admit that things could be better between Grace and me. Almost immediately, a question popped into my mind: Was my resistance getting in the way of listening openly to what he had to offer? No matter. It was time to bite the bullet. I had to try what he had to offer. What choice did I have? I was desperate.

"Let's be clear about this," Joseph said. "This system of tools and practices is not psychotherapy, but you can think of it as learning how to coach yourself through challenges to get better results. It's about becoming more efficient, productive, creative, and successful, and it's about leading others toward those ends," Joseph continued, "and I think you'll agree there's nothing more practical than that. In the end, I believe you'll be able to make a quantum leap out of your present dilemma. Despite any doubts you might have at the present time, I'm with Alexa on this one. I'm betting on your success."

At this point Joseph declared a half-hour intermission, as he jokingly called it. I made a quick call back to my office. There was nothing that couldn't wait, which was a relief. I was feeling pretty shaken up.

When I left Joseph's office, I headed for a quiet coffee shop to look over his Users Guide and think about my next moves. Did Joseph understand my strengths as an answer man? Was I missing something? Was he?

Minutes later, standing in the mirrored elevator, I looked up and caught my reflection. Staring back at me was the face of a stranger filled with tension and frustration—me! Was this the face that Grace had been looking at for the past few months? Truth be told, I wasn't sure I'd want to hang around that guy myself. Could I really change, as Alexa and Joseph seemed to believe? And did I really want to? Maybe I should accept my strengths as a guy who's an expert on answers. Maybe I had to start asking myself some hard questions about what I wanted for myself. What if I really wasn't leadership material?

CHAPTER 3

The Choice Map

"Maps don't just help us locate where we are but where we are coming from and where we might be going."

Gabrielle Roth

When we resumed our conversation, Joseph pointed to a mural on his office wall. I'd noticed it before but hadn't paid much attention to it (see Figure 1). "This is the Choice Map," he explained. "It helps us become better observers of the two basic paths we take in life—the Learner Mindset path and the Judger Mindset path. As the name implies, the map is all about our ability to make choices.

On the left side of the Choice Map, notice the figure standing above the Start arrow, at the crossroads between the two paths. That figure represents you and me—every one of us. In every moment of our lives, we're faced with choosing between the Learner Mindset path and the Judger Mindset path. Now look at the thought bubbles above the figures' heads. Note how there's a relationship between the kinds of questions these figures ask, the path they're on, and where each path takes them."

Joseph then directed my attention to two little signs near that Start arrow on the left of the map: The sign above the Learner Mindset path said "Choose"; the sign by the Judger Mindset path

Figure 1. The Choice Map

Readers can download a free color copy of the Choice Map at www.inquiryinstitute.com

said "React." I looked at the Learner Mindset path with the figures happily jogging along. That path, associated with choosing,
looked pretty inviting to me.

I then looked at the Judger Mindset path, with the sign that
said React. The figures there looked downright troubled and bleak
as the path took them toward the billboard labeled Judger. No
happy joggers here. And then I noticed that fellow sinking in the
mud of the Judger Pit. I started to chuckle but then swallowed
hard. Was this Joseph's impression of me? My shoulders tightened
up. What if he was right?

"I hope you're not thinking I'm like that loser in the Judger
Pit," I said guardedly.

"You wouldn't be in this office if anybody believed you were a
loser," Joseph replied. "Every single one of us has Judger moments,
including me. It's a natural part of being human. The Choice Map
is about observing yourself and others in a more conscious way; it's
about helping us to see what mindset path we're on at any moment.
It's not about labeling people or putting them in boxes. Think of
the Choice Map as a self-coaching tool that helps us to be more
aware, and that helps us chart more effective paths through our
lives—and for getting better outcomes in whatever we do."

I began to relax a little.

"At nearly every moment of our lives, we're faced with choosing between taking the Learner or Judger path," Joseph continued.
"We're making choices moment by moment by moment though
we don't always recognize it. Many of our choices may be embod-
ied within routines or habits we've developed over the years, some
of them so necessary in our everyday lives that we barely notice

they were once choices. As an example, maybe you've always taken a certain route because it was the quickest way to work. Then, traffic patterns change and the old route takes twice as long. Instead of finding a new route, you continue to take the old one. When someone suggests a better route, you defend your old one, complaining about the heavy traffic and congestion. How we choose to handle the change takes us along the Learner path or the Judger path. These are our mindsets. As you can see, by choosing Learner mindset we can discover new possibilities. By jumping into Judger mindset, we can eventually end up stuck in the mud—or following an old route that is as uncomfortable as it is unproductive.

"Most of the time, we're shifting back and forth between Learner and Judger mindsets, barely aware we have any control or choice. Much of what we experience can just seem true or real or logical to us. We go along as if what we experience is the way things are. Real choice begins when we are mindful enough to observe our own thoughts and feelings as well as the language we use to express them. This is the key to success—it's like a gym for our brains rather than our muscles. Self-coaching is impossible without a strong self-observer! It's as simple as asking ourselves, What's going on? Where am I right now? Am I in Judger or Learner? What do I want? Choice begins with observing our own thinking, our emotions, and our mindsets. It's simpler than you think."

I nodded, feeling a little less skeptical.

"Let's put it to the test," Joseph said. "We've got a perfect issue to work with, too. Look at what happened in that moment when you asked if I thought you were a loser and a Judger."

"Okay," I said, nodding uneasily.

"Imagine that it's you standing at the crossroads between the Learner and Judger paths," Joseph said, pointing to that Start arrow on the left of the Choice Map. "Notice the words that circle that figure's head—Anything that impacts us at any moment. That can be Thoughts, Feelings, Circumstances. The circumstances might be something unpleasant, such as getting an unexpected bill or a phone call with distressing news. Maybe a truck scraped the fender of your new car in the parking lot. The whole world begins to look like that mud pit at the end of the Judger path. Stuff happens. Right?"

I rolled my eyes and thought, he doesn't know the half of it!

"But circumstances that feel positive impact us, too," Joseph continued. "Your favorite team has an unexpected win. Your boss gives you a promotion, or your spouse sends an invitation to spend a romantic evening together."

"I could stand more of the good stuff!" I grumbled. "So, what's the point here?"

"Things happen to us all the time," Joseph said. "We don't have much choice about that but we do have choice about how we interpret what just happened and what we decide to do next. Case in point: let's examine what happened the exact moment when I first showed you the Choice Map. Just looking at it led to thoughts and feelings that put you on the Judger Mindset path. What do you think happened?"

"I don't know," I said. "Something just pushed my buttons and off I went." I remembered the questions that ran through my mind at that moment: Does Joseph think I'm a Judger and a loser?

Does he think I'm like that guy in the Judger Pit sinking in the mud?

"Yeah, I admit it," I said. "I went into a pretty bad mindset."

"Whoa!" Joseph exclaimed. "There's no good or bad, no right or wrong here. There's just observing what happens and what you do with what happens. Remember the little signs at the beginning of the paths—Choose and React. In those first instants, you reacted to what happened and bombarded yourself with negative Judger questions."

"Am I a hopeless case?" I said, cracking a feeble smile.

Joseph smiled back. "That's a good example of a negative Self-Question, or Self-Q, as I call them, which sends us right into the Judger Pit."

"So how do I get out?"

"You observe your mindset and then choose. I believe that a secret of being effective and satisfied in our lives begins with our ability to distinguish between Judger and Learner. That's a key part of Question Thinking. Change your questions, change your thinking. Change your thinking, change your results. If only for a second, you can stand back and become an observer watching a movie of your life. You simply notice whatever moods, thoughts, and behaviors are going on, without interpretation or judgment. That mindfulness sets the stage for just accepting what is, which also sets the stage for change, for recognizing that we do have a choice about the mindset we're operating from. This is very different from being so immersed in the situation that we can't imagine anything other than what already is. And it's a sure way of releasing ourselves from those feelings of being a puppet whose strings are pulled by other people or by circumstances beyond our control."

I nodded. "With engineering problems, I use something like this observer self to cross-check my calculations and conclusions and make sure I haven't missed anything. You're saying the Choice Map gives me a way of developing this observer self to cross-check myself—to observe whatever moods and thoughts might be shaping my choices—not just about numbers but also about myself and other people. That gives me the power to make a course correction."

"Exactly! I'm sure you've had the experience of catching yourself calling somebody by the wrong name or nearly putting your foot in your mouth. We all do it. It's your observer self that catches the error. You see, it's a natural capacity, something everyone has—and using the Choice Map gives us a chance to focus on the bigger picture. Until you develop this ability you're running on automatic pilot, reacting mindlessly. The Choice Map is about developing ways to make intentional, conscious choices rather than being controlled by events around us or by our emotions. These are essential leadership qualities for being aware, awake, and responsive to the business at hand."

Joseph paused. Then his face broke into a smile. "Let me tell you a little story about myself," he said. "A few months ago, I was in a coaching session with the superintendent of a large construction company. I spent 15 long minutes listening to his complaining and blaming all his company's woes on everybody else. He kept saying the world is filled with idiots. I was getting pretty fed up with all his judgmental chatter. I felt like kicking him out of my office! Judger questions were coursing wildly through my mind. What did I do to deserve this guy? Who does he think he is, God's gift to mankind? When I suddenly realized what I was doing I almost laughed out loud. Here I was judging this man for judging other people! I was in Judger mindset as much as he was. I'd been hijacked by Judger!"

Joseph obviously enjoyed telling this story on himself. "So how did the Choice Map help?" I wanted him to tell me the whole process.

"First, you just notice that something's not quite right," he said. "Maybe you feel tense, or upset, or just plain blocked. That's your observer self clicking in, making you more aware. Your body gives you the loudest clues, often before your mind does. You suddenly realize your shoulders are up around your ears, or maybe your stomach growls. Then you ask yourself, Am I in Judger? If the answer is Yes, you can ask yourself, Is this where I want to be? Of course, in the story I'm telling you, the answer to that question was no. If I'd stayed in Judger, no way could I help that guy. No one can help anyone else from a Judger place."

> No one can help anyone else from a Judger place.

"Sounds like you should have cut your losses and backed out," I suggested.

"Not at all," Joseph replied. "As soon as our observer self recognizes we're in Judger, that's when we begin to gain control and personal power. Of course, we have to recognize Judger non-judgmentally. That's true whether we're in Judger about ourselves or about someone else. This gives us choice about what we do next. We can choose to switch our thinking from Judger to Learner. There's a specific kind of question I call a Switching question which provides the how-to for changing. The Switching question that worked for me that day was, how else can I think about him?

"That question gave me the freedom to wonder: What does he need? Instead of wanting to write him off, that question helped me become curious about him. The Choice Map simplifies this whole process for observing yourself. You discover more options and can choose more wisely, even under pressure. Choosing is easy when things are going well. It's when we're under pressure that we really get tested."

Something in what he said made me think about that awful moment with Grace at the airport. "It seems like whenever there's conflict, Judger is involved," I reflected. "I mean, both people end up in Judger. That's pretty normal, isn't it?"

"Very normal," Joseph said. "And when that happens, everything escalates, and the possibility of a good resolution comes to a screeching halt. But here's a million-dollar tip for you: Whenever two people find themselves in conflict, whoever wakes up to their own Judger has the ability to turn the situation around."

> Whenever two people find themselves
> in conflict, whoever wakes up to their own Judger
> has the ability to turn the situation around.

Something clicked for me. When Grace and I had a disagreement, she would often switch from stubbornness to open-mindedness in the blink of an eye. Her ability to switch always lightened things up. I had often wondered if she did this naturally or if it was some inner trick. She once told me she just took a deep breath and reminded herself of the big picture—that our relationship was more important than proving she was right. If Joseph's techniques could teach me how to do this by choice, I'd be way ahead of the game with Charles, my nemesis at work.

"I'm willing to give it a try," I told Joseph cautiously. "Where do I begin?"

"You begin with noticing a body feeling, sometimes a very subtle one, like a slight tightness in your jaw, or in your shoulders, or you get what you might call a gut feeling."

"Yeah," I said. "I do get my hackles up. I guess you'd call that defensive."

"At that point it's helpful to notice the questions you're asking yourself. What's the mindset you're asking from? Am I in Judger? Asking those questions is critical. We're most effective and satisfied with virtually everything we do when we're in Learner. That's when we're most resourceful, resilient, and flexible and have the most options.

"But don't worry if you take the Judger path every once in a while. That's just human. We all do it. Even after all these years of mindset practice, I still go Judger several times a day. At least now I laugh at myself and don't go Judger on my own Judger.

"As your observer self gets stronger and more dependable, you'll find it increasingly easy to switch your questions and get back in Learner. That's where things open up again and you go toward the results you're seeking."

"You make it sound so easy," I said.

"It's easier than you think," Joseph said, "because everything you need is already built in. Continually asking Switching questions is what helps us to build a resilient observer self and a robust Learner mindset. You're developing the ability for defusing Judger and the messes it can create.

Continually asking Switching questions
is what helps us to build a resilient observer
self and a robust Learner mindset.

"The signals for catching yourself in Judger are difficult to argue with, since they're your body's reactions and your moods. Remember what happened to me with the superintendent? The clues that I was in Judger were in my own moods and attitudes, which I've learned to associate with Judger—self-righteousness, arrogance, anger, and defensiveness. For example, you might be thinking, I sure showed that guy! Or, Maybe that'll teach him to listen to me next time. Or, what an idiot that so-and-so is! I've learned that any time I get into negative moods, Judger questions and attitudes are involved. Once I observe this state in myself, I can change my questions and turn things around pretty easily, and get a very different result."

He paused for a moment, then said, "Let's do an experiment. I'm going to recite two different sets of questions. As I do, notice how each set of questions affects you. Pay attention to your breathing, your muscles, your posture, and what you're feeling in different areas of your body. "He got up and walked over to the Choice Map. "Ask yourself these questions:

What's wrong with me?

Whose fault is it?

Why am I such a failure?

Why can't I ever do anything right?

Why are they so clueless and frustrating?

Haven't we already been there, done that?

Why bother?"

As he recited these questions (see Figure 2), my chest tightened up. My shoulders stiffened. I was clutching up like a rookie pitcher in the last inning of an important game. I laughed uncomfortably, "Yeah, I definitely feel some tension here and there."

"Okay. How would you describe how you feel?"

I shrugged. "To be honest," I said. "I feel like that guy in the Judger Pit." I grappled for words to describe what I was feeling. Finally, I came up with: Hopeless and helpless. Pessimistic. Negative. Depleted. Depressed. Uptight. Victim. Loser. I was relieved Joseph didn't insist I share everything going on with me.

"Now give yourself a moment or two to breathe and just observe whatever is going on with you right now. Imagine you're

Learner/Judger Questions	
Judger	**Learner**
What's wrong with me?	What do I value about myself?
What's wrong with him/her?	What do I appreciate about him/her?
Whose fault is it?	Am I being responsible?
How can I prove I'm right?	What can I learn? What's useful?
Why are they so clueless and frustrating?	What are they thinking, feeling, and wanting?
Haven't we been there, done that?	What are the best steps forward?
Why bother?	What's possible?

Figure 2. Learner/Judger Questions

an observer watching yourself sitting here in my office. As you do this also notice if any feelings and sensations start to shift."

I did what he said. The changes were subtle at first. It seemed like those negative sensations were starting to diminish. I nodded. "Yes. I like that," I said.

"That's just a taste of the power of self-coaching and how the observer self serves that process," Joseph said. "Later on, we'll explore more about tools for strengthening your observer self. You'll be able to zero in on the kinds of questions that get you stuck, and you'll learn to craft new questions that launch you right up into Learner territory. This is fundamental for a leader because a leader's mood plays a huge factor in whether they'll be successful or not. A friend of mine had a very clever way of saying this: 'Either you have your questions, or your questions have you.'"

> Either you have your questions,
> or your questions have you.

Joseph strode easily around the room, stroking his chin as if he were considering something. Finally, he stopped and faced me again. "How about checking out the Learner path," he asked. "Again, listen to the questions as if you were asking them of yourself:

What happened?

What do I want?

What's useful about this?

What can I learn?

What's the other person thinking, feeling, and wanting?

What are my choices?

What's best to do now?

What's possible?"

With these questions I experienced a quiet excitement, very different from what I'd experienced with the Judger questions. My breathing got easier. My mood got lighter. I suddenly had more energy. I sensed a willingness and openness I certainly hadn't felt with the first set of questions. My shoulders relaxed. What a surprise. I hadn't felt this calm in a while! I was amazed at how quickly my mood had changed.

"What are some words you'd use to describe your experience now?" he asked.

I took a deep, easy breath. "Open. Lighter. Upbeat. Curious. Energetic. Optimistic." I chuckled. "I'm a damn-sight more hopeful than I felt this morning...maybe there are solutions to my problems after all."

"Good," Joseph said. "Those feelings signal that you've stepped into Learner mindset. You're on the Learner path."

I heaved a sigh of relief. Even if I wasn't totally sold on everything Joseph was saying, maybe there was something to this coaching after all. I had to admit I was feeling more hopeful than I'd felt in a long time. Could it be that this guy actually was as good as Alexa seemed to believe he was? Despite that big question mark on his business card, maybe he did have tools that could make a difference for me...as nutty as that might seem.

CHAPTER 4

We're All Recovering Judgers

"There is a crucial difference between being caught up in a feeling and becoming aware that you are being swept away by it. Socrates' injunction 'know thyself' speaks to this keystone of emotional intelligence: awareness of one's own feelings as they occur."

Daniel Goleman

We took a short break while Joseph went off to get us fresh coffee from the kitchenette adjacent to his office. He was gone long enough for me to check my phone. There was a voice message from Grace. It was about her young assistant, Jennifer, who had messed up on yet another assignment. "I've just got to vent," Grace was saying. "I feel like I'm two seconds from firing her. Can you call me right back?" I clicked off my phone. Why was Grace bothering me at work? Couldn't she handle Jennifer by herself? Did she think I needed her problems on top of mine? My jaw and shoulders clenched up.

Just then Joseph returned with a tray that held two full coffee mugs and containers of cream and sugar. I took a mug, glad for the simple distraction. I needed to settle myself down so I could listen to what Joseph was starting to tell me. He was back to his story about the superintendent.

"My client and I both had a breakthrough that day," he was saying, "right after I recognized I had gotten hijacked by Judger."

"Wait a second," I said. "You used that term before—getting highjacked by Judger. What's a Judger highjack?"

"It's when something happens that triggers you, pushes your buttons. It's usually a person or some situation." Joseph said. "You're going along with the best of intentions and suddenly you feel yourself tensing up, going Judger, and pretty soon you're not listening at all. You're getting increasingly defensive, or you just want to run out of the room screaming."

"I know the feeling," I said. "I know it only too well. But isn't that pretty normal?"

"Normal, yes," Joseph said. "The problem is that normal or not, if we want to get things accomplished, we've got to have tools for recovering ourselves, getting centered, and giving our thinking brain a chance to lead. That's switching into Learner mindset. Once we've done that, our perspective will change and open up. That's how you recover from a Judger hijack."

"That's all well and good," I said. "But did you ever get through to that superintendent guy? Did he ever get it?" The minute I asked that question I realized I'd been asking that same question about myself: Did I get it? Something about that superintendent's story was making me uneasy. But what was it?

"Oh, sure. The superintendent eventually got it," Joseph said. "In the end, he made an interesting comment. "With the 'Judger agenda,' as he called it, 'the costs can be tremendous. The future can only be a recycled version of the past. If you're working from the Learner program the power is on. The juice is flowing. You can make a new future for yourself.'"

With the "Judger agenda," the costs can be tremendous. The future can only be a recycled version of the past. If you're working from the Learner program the power is on. The juice is flowing. You can make a new future for yourself.

Suddenly I knew what was bugging me. That story about the superintendent could actually be about me.

"You make it sound like any kind of judgment is a bad thing," I interrupted. "But I disagree. I could never do my job without making judgments…and I take a lot of pride in making good ones. You have to judge when you're making technological choices, or when you're choosing a vendor to buy from, or whether you're assigning the best person to do a certain job."

"By all means," Joseph said. "You bring up an important point. Exercising judgment is about thinking things through and making informed choices. I call that discernment which is essential in a job like yours. The point is that I'm not talking about judgment in that sense of the word. I'm talking about being judgmental, as in fault-finding or being critical or dwelling on the negative. Remember, Judger means judgmental. Being judgmental and having good judgment are two very different things.

"In fact, Judger mindset is the enemy of good judgment. When we're judgmental, brain activity gets spikey; the big muscles of our bodies prepare themselves for fighting or running. In some cases, we freeze; our brains just shut down and it becomes difficult to think at all. It's the classic fight-or-flight response, with all our energies going in the direction of running away, putting up a good fight…or shutting down in resignation or defeat. Those are all variations of our survival mode responses. Using good judgment is the opposite of all this. It's a shame those words—judgment and judgmental—even sound alike. One of my dictionaries defines judgmental as 'attacking self or others.' Nothing could be more different from exercising good judgment."

Judger mindset is the enemy of good judgment.

"I get it. So, Judger always means judgmental," I said.

"That's right," Joseph said, taking a sip of coffee, "Judger is always judgmental. What's more, Judger has two faces—either we're being judgmental toward ourselves or we're being judgmental toward other people. And sometimes we're actually doing both."

I fell silent, trying to absorb what he was telling me. How did it apply to me? I'd certainly gotten judgmental when I listened to Grace's message. I'd jumped right into Judger. But her calling me at work about Jennifer wasn't exactly using the best judgment on Grace's part, either. Or was I being judgmental about Grace, too?

Joseph settled back into his chair. "What's going through your mind right now?" he asked.

"I can't deny that I've been spending a lot of time in Judger lately," I began hesitantly. "But how do you avoid going down that path when you've got a guy like Charles to deal with? He's the main source of the problems with our team and our miserable results. He's driving me nuts." I clamped my jaw shut, not wanting to say anything more. I didn't like thinking about myself as being so much in Judger. In fact, I was really starting to resent this Judger stuff. Besides, how do you stay on the Learner path with problems piling up all around you?

Joseph must have read my mind because the next thing he said was, "Remember that slipping into Judger is just part of being human, especially when things aren't going well. Judger will always be part of you and everyone else, too. In this respect, we're all recovering Judgers. The goal is to develop a whole new relationship with Judger. You might even say a Learner relationship. No doubt about it, our Judger reactiveness can be a bit addictive and it's easy to get over-attached to our Judger opinions. The more we indulge in Judger, the more it becomes a habit and takes over. While it's true we can never get rid of Judger, we can learn to manage it, to just accept and be with it. Once you do that a whole new way of being becomes available. Awareness, commitment, compassion, courage, forgiveness, acceptance—with a dash of humor—that's what it takes to keep recovering ourselves and resetting our course back to the Learner path.

"The whole idea is to accept Judger and practice Learner, moment by moment by moment. This work is not about getting on the Learner path and staying there. That's a pipe dream. Real personal power depends on how quickly we can get good at recovering from Judger once it takes over. That's why I got such a kick out of that situation with my superintendent client. Sure, I got hijacked by Judger, but the instant I realized it, I could rescue myself and get my power back by stepping onto the Learner path. Sometimes it's even fun to see how fast I can catch Judger and how easily I can recover.

> The whole idea is to accept Judger and practice Learner, moment by moment by moment.

"Frankly," Joseph said with a smile, "sometimes I find myself slipping into Judger several times an hour!"

"That's difficult to believe. You're pretty good at hiding it."

"It's not about hiding. I always say, Judger denied is Judger squared. Judger gets bigger if we deny it. Rather than hiding Judger, I've worked hard at creating a friendly relationship with it. This begins with acceptance, real acceptance, which is very different than just tolerating some person or situation. By the way, in your Users Guide you'll find a tool called Make Friends with Judger."

"That means accepting and making peace with my own Judger," I said. "Is that what you mean by creating a friendly relationship with Judger?"

"I would add that whenever you can accept others when they're in Judger, that can often help them change too.'

What he proposed was really testing me. I thought to myself, He wants me to accept being Judger towards myself. Did that include accepting my being so Judger about Charles? I recalled a dinner that Grace and I had with her cousin the week before. He shared something very personal. He had been struggling with a drinking problem. Things had gotten so bad that he finally started going to AA meetings. Thankfully, he was now doing much better. Her cousin said that one thing that really had helped him was the Serenity Prayer. 'God grant me the serenity to accept the things I cannot change, the courage to change the things I can, and the wisdom to know the difference.'

Was Joseph saying that I cannot change having a Judger mindset, but I can change what I do about it, including how I relate to other people? The idea of having to deal with Judger forever didn't please me very much. On the other hand, at least it meant I wasn't any worse off than anyone else. I pictured Grace smiling at the idea!

I guess I had drifted off a bit, putting these ideas together in my mind. Suddenly I heard Joseph asking me, "Can you tell me a little more about Charles?"

"He's second in command on the project team I head up," I said, hoping my exasperation didn't show too much. "But this guy challenges everything I say. I must admit, he's probably got a legitimate bone to pick with me. He was passed over for the position I got, and boy, does he resent it. I would, too, if I were in his shoes! He's a real know-it-all, picky and petty. He asks so many questions. It's like one interruption after another. He's out to sabotage me. That's the bottom line. And it looks like he's succeeding."

"When you think about Charles, what's the first question that pops into your mind?"

I chuckled. "That's easy! How can I put a leash on this guy before he destroys me?"

"Anything else?"

"Lots of things! How can I stay in control? Aren't I supposed to be the one who's the leader of this team? How can I make this guy get with the program?"

"And?"

"How did I ever get myself into this mess? Whatever made me think I could handle being a leader?" I paused for a moment, then asserted, "Listen, the thing is, Charles needs to change as much as you seem to think I do."

"What you're saying about Charles may be true," Joseph said. "But you're the one in my office now. Change begins with the person who wants the change. Right?"

That really knocked the wind out of my sails. I sat back in my chair and took a deep breath. "What am I supposed to do, ignore the fact that he stabs me in the back every chance he gets?" I was getting steamed. "There's no way to separate my reactions from what Charles does!"

"Ah, but that's the beauty of it," Joseph said. "You can separate your reactions from his behavior—and anyone else's. Until you do, you'll keep giving away your power. Anybody, including Charles, will be able to pull your strings and hijack your Judger. It's a matter of whether you have your Judger or your Judger has you."

Either you have your Judger or your Judger has you.

"I'm not agreeing or disagreeing with you," I said, secretly seething inside. "I don't think I could possibly see this situation with Charles any differently."

"Is that a question?" Joseph asked.

"What are you saying?"

"Can you reshape that statement as a question?"

"You mean, like, how else can I think about this?" To my surprise, the moment I asked myself this question I felt a subtle shift inside. For one thing, I let go of the breath I hadn't even known I was holding, and my shoulders relaxed enough that Joseph probably saw it.

"Exactly. Did you notice? You just switched yourself into Learner. Quick as that. And here's my answer: No matter what Charles or anyone else might do, you can use the Choice Map, and what you're learning about your body's messages, to identify when you've gone into Judger. You've heard that expression— What matters isn't what happens to you in life. What matters is what you do next. The Choice Map reminds us to stand back and observe where we are so we can have a choice about what to do next. You empower your observer self, like watching your own movie for a moment. Then you'll be able to tell the difference between what Charles does and what you choose to do with what he does. You get to ask one of my favorite Switching questions, 'Who do I choose to be in this moment?'"

I tried to take in Joseph's lesson. It wasn't easy. Judger questions were still running through my brain and my body could feel them, too. I guess Judger had a grip on me where Charles was concerned. Could that be true in my marriage, too?

"Let's go back for a moment to that figure standing at the crossroads," Joseph said, tapping his finger on the Start arrow on the left side of the Choice Map. "Remember, this figure represents every one of us at the moment when we're hit with something and we have to deal with it. It could be some circumstance outside us, or it could be our own thoughts and feelings. We're stumped. Regardless of the situation, it's vital to remember we have choice about how to respond. Do you know what those choices are?"

"We can just react and jump right into Judger," I said, feeling my way along, "Or we can pause, check in with our moods and body feelings, and notice what kinds of questions we're asking, then try to choose Learner. We can choose…we really do have choice."

Fireworks started going off in my mind. I actually do have choice! And I can choose Learner when I want to. Maybe Joseph's methods really could make a difference with my results at work.

"I have to say," I told him cautiously, "maybe it's not as difficult to distinguish between Judger and Learner as I thought."

Joseph actually clapped his hands. "Yes. Yes, that's great! Once you're able to observe your own thoughts and feelings, and recognize the differences between Learner and Judger, you step into self-coaching territory, where you grab hold of the power of choice. The very essence of our humanness is our ability not only to choose between one thing and another but to create new choices."

Joseph seemed tremendously excited by this notion. "You're a quick study," he exclaimed. "I see another of the traits Alexa values in you so much." He glanced at his wristwatch. "We've been talking for a long time. Let's stop here for the day."

Joseph opened a drawer in his desk and took out some color-
ful copies of the Choice Map.

"Take these with you," he said, handing them to me. "Study
the Choice Map when you get to your office. And take one home
to post on your refrigerator."

I groaned inwardly. What on earth would I tell Grace about
all this! She'd want to know where I'd gotten the Choice Map and
why I'd put it on the refrigerator.

"This map illustrates fundamental distinctions between
Learner and Judger mindsets," Joseph said, as we walked down the
hall. "Ultimately, the message is pretty simple. Change your questions, change your results. This is core self-management know-
how for every recovering Judger. And that applies for all of us.
We're all recovering Judgers." Joseph laughed. "Recognizing this
helps me stay humble."

Change your questions, change your results.

At the doors of his outer office, Joseph stopped and turned
to face me. Over his shoulder, on the wall with the Question
Thinking Hall of Fame, I spotted a picture of Alexa. It appeared
to be from a major magazine, profiling her for some award.
Embarrassed though I was to admit it, I hadn't known about this
article or her award. Given how long I'd known Alexa, I certainly
should have known that.

"I'll see you next time," Joseph said, shaking my hand warmly.

My head was spinning. My whole life was being turned upside down. What really puzzled me was that I also felt lighter, more optimistic than I'd been in ages. One thing Alexa was right about—this Joseph guy had a provocative way of looking at how to make changes in our lives. I began to imagine that maybe, by working with him, I'd come up with answers—or was it new questions—that could put my career back on track.

CHAPTER 5

Kitchen Talk

"The big question is whether you are going to be able
to say a hearty yes to your adventure."

Joseph Campbell

It was early in the morning when Grace found the Choice Map
I had stuck on the refrigerator door the night before. As usual, I
awoke to the smell of fresh coffee and made my way downstairs
to the kitchen. Grace is always up before me. She's one of those
people who wakes up cheerful and enthusiastic about each new
day. I'm just the opposite, and I know it sometimes puts Grace on
edge. She claims that I'm like a bear coming out of hibernation in
the morning. I don't think I'm quite that bad, but I don't exactly
start the day off with a song in my heart.

As I entered the kitchen, I found Grace standing in front of
the refrigerator with her back to me. She appeared to be engrossed
with the Choice Map. I was immediately worried about what she
might say. I was pretty sure she'd start probing, and I'd have to tell
her the whole thing—about my trouble at work and all the rest of
it. That would lead to how I'd gotten the Choice Map and why I'd
posted it on the refrigerator. Then I might have to tell her about

why Alexa had referred me to Joseph, and that could turn into an emotional minefield.

While I was worrying about how I would avoid telling her the whole story, Grace suddenly turned around and gave me a big hug.

"Where did you get this?" she asked. "It's terrific!"

She took the Choice Map off the refrigerator door and started waving it around in her hand. I mumbled something about it being a handout for a special training at work, and then poured a cup of coffee for myself and one for Grace.

"I'm amazed," she said. "I've already learned something from this. You remember that message I left you about Jennifer, my assistant at work? I guess I've been riding her pretty hard lately. I can just feel her cringing any time I get within a few feet of her. Looking at the Choice Map, I realize I've been very Judger with her, like it says here, and I'm sure that's put her on edge. She's been messing up a lot, but this makes me wonder if I've been contributing to the problem. After all, nobody does their best work when their boss is expecting the worst from them."

"It's all in the kinds of questions you ask." I didn't even think before the words just popped out of my mouth.

"What questions?" Grace asked. "I don't ever get that far with poor Jennifer."

"According to this guy Joseph, who gave me this map…"

"Wait," Grace interrupted. "Who's Joseph?"

I stared at her blankly for a moment, debating about whether to tell her the truth. I decided to keep things simple. "He's this consultant Alexa hired," I told her, determined not to go into any more details than absolutely necessary. Yesterday, right after meeting with Joseph, I'd spent an hour studying the map, preparing answers for any questions Grace might have. "He claims that most of the time we're not even aware of the questions we ask ourselves or other people. That's what the Choice Map teaches. It's a reminder to look carefully at those questions, because they affect how we think, feel, and act and even how other people respond to us."

Grace looked puzzled. I pressed close to her and pointed to the figure at the crossroads. "There's the key right there," I said, pointing to the words Thoughts, Feelings, Circumstances near the figure's head. "The moment anything happens to us, that's when we start asking ourselves questions. The sooner we recognize what we're asking, the better. That way we have more options." Was this really me talking? I was amazed at how much I recalled of Joseph's teachings. The more we talked, the more comfortable I was getting with this QT stuff.

"The main thing I see are these two paths," Grace said, tracing first one and then the other with her finger. "Take the Learner route and you'll move right along. The Learner guy is saying, 'What do I want? What are my choices?' This other one is asking, 'What can I learn?' Oh, you're right, these are all questions. And the guy on the Judger path, he's all caught up with different questions like: 'Whose fault is it? What's wrong with them?' I'll tell you, Ben, at the office, every time I hear a pin drop or somebody sigh, the first thing that pops into my head is, 'Oh, Lord, what's wrong now? What else can Jennifer possibly mess up?' And then, in a flash, I'm down on her. Do you know what she did yesterday,

Ben? She…oh, hold it. That's taking me right into Judger territory, isn't it?"

"The way it works," I explained, "is that from moment to moment, stuff happens. Good stuff and bad stuff. It sort of hits us unawares. Then, especially if we have a strong Judger habit, our questions tend to follow that same pattern. If we're more in Learner mode, we'll ask questions in that direction."

"Action follows thought," Grace added. "It's a basic principle. But I never thought about it in terms of questions. Action follows questions. Seems to me the trick is to just keep ourselves in a Learner frame of mind."

"According to Joseph," I told Grace, "Nobody stays in Learner all the time. It's natural to slip into Judger now and then. In fact, we alternate between the two mindsets all the time. It's just human nature." Even as I said those words, I was thinking about the argument she and I got into that day I dropped her off at the airport. I was still feeling embarrassed about how I'd treated her. I wasn't ready to go into all that with Grace, but at least I summoned up the nerve to mention part of it.

"It's so easy to go into Judger," I said, carefully choosing my words. "For example, the other day I was trying to pull out into traffic and nearly got hit by a taxi that was going about twice the speed it should have. I instantly went into Judger. It was like a bolt of lightning, you know? It happened that fast. In an instant, I was ready to punch the guy out."

"Sometimes you really worry me," Grace said, shaking her head.

My shoulders tensed up and I could feel myself getting defensive. I knew she didn't approve of my driving habits, though I'd never had an accident. We'd gotten into arguments about this before, but this time a part of me stopped and said, Don't go there, buddy. I took a deep breath, shrugged my shoulders, and just tried to keep things easy and relaxed.

"It's just an example. What I now see, thanks to Joseph's Choice Map, is how that close call immediately put me in Judger. I'm not saying I handled it well. In fact, I know I didn't, because I was angry as hell for the next couple of hours. I was experiencing what Joseph calls a Judger hijack."

I really wanted to tell Grace the whole story, about how I'd lumped together everything I'd been experiencing lately. I'd been stewing about whether to resign. I was irritated about having to meet with Joseph. I was hurt, worried about my whole career going up in smoke, and angry with Grace for pressuring me about our relationship in the midst of all this. My life had become just one big...well, one big Judger Pit, I guess, and I had been sinking in the mud.

I tensed all over as I realized I'd been as much of a challenge to Joseph as that judgmental superintendent he'd told me about. That first day I'd slouched into his office certain that meeting with him was going to be a hopeless waste of my time. In the mood I'd been in, it was a miracle anything he said had gotten through to me. Now I was telling Grace about Joseph's ideas as if I actually knew what I was talking about!

"I'm thinking this map is a good reminder of what happens to me when I get stuck in one of my Judger heads," Grace said. She turned away for a moment and sat down at the breakfast table. She sipped her coffee and nibbled her toast as she studied the map.

I continued standing, leaning against the counter, watching her. After a moment, Grace looked up a little shyly.

"Maybe this could help us...you know, in our relationship," she said. "What do you think?" There was not the slightest hint of blame or judgment in her voice. I was really grateful for that.

"Joseph says that life is filled with those moments when something hits us and sets us off on one path or another...."

"But what do you think," Grace asked, "I mean, about it helping us—you and me?"

This time I thought I detected a bit of an edge in her voice. She really wanted me to tell her exactly what I was thinking. "As I said," I answered. "I think it applies well to any and all areas of our lives. We can all use better tools."

"What's that supposed to mean, better tools?" she asked, sounding definitely irritated.

I tried to ignore Grace's eyes. So far our conversation had gone so well, I didn't want it to turn sour. I was already asking myself: What stupid thing did I say to mess things up again? And why did she bring up our relationship in the first place? Talk about bad timing! And then I caught myself. Those simple little questions were pushing me right down the Judger path. This time, though, I saw it coming. I imagined Joseph as a coach on the sidelines shouting to me, Learner! Learner! Remember the Choice Map! Change your questions! You can turn this around! Almost instantly a new question occurred to me: How can I keep things positive between Grace and me?

"Sorry," Grace was saying. "I just realized I was starting to go Judger on you."

For a moment I felt puzzled, then relieved as it dawned on me what had happened. Grace had started going down the Judger path. We both had. And then she stopped herself, and so did I. Amazing! In spite of myself, I smiled.

"What are you smiling about?" Grace asked. She got up from the table, took her dishes to the sink, then turned to face me.

"Sweetheart," I said. "You're wonderful!" I took her in my arms and held her close. She stiffened but quickly softened and hugged me back.

"Do you remember that night when we had dinner at the Metropol and I was late?" I asked. I felt her nodding her head against my shoulder.

"We really got into it, didn't we, about who got their times mixed up? Then you did a remarkable thing. You suddenly just dropped the whole argument, and everything shifted. We got connected again. Do you remember?"

"Mm hmm, I sure do!" She chuckled, planting a kiss on my cheek.

It was difficult being serious while remembering that night, but I really wanted to get my point across. "Joseph talks about switching from Judger to Learner, and how we can do that with a single question."

"Like when I ask myself: Do I want to win this argument? Or do I want to us to be closer, like we are now?" Grace drew away from me but kept her hands on my shoulders.

"Is that how you do your magic?" I asked.

"Some of it," she said, leaning into me again. "But I never thought of it in terms of questions."

"I'm serious," I said, wanting to make certain I got my point across. "I just realized that you're a natural at the very thing Joseph teaches. I'll bet you do it by changing your questions, even if you're not aware of it. You take yourself straight to Learner. That's how you shift your mood!"

"I like those shifts!"

"Me, too," I said, hugging her again. I still wanted to know more about how she made those shifts. "How did you learn to do that?"

Grace thought for a moment. Her face lit up like she'd just remembered something that delighted her. Then she said, "When I was about eight or ten, I was all upset because I'd just had a big argument with my best friend. I was so angry! My mom was really worried about me. She sat down beside me and told me this story about the two wolves. As the story goes, this wise old man is telling his grandson about life. He tells him that we each have two wolves who live within us. One represents anger, jealousy, greed, selfishness, hate, self-pity, guilt, resentment, lies, you know, all those things that seem to be at the center of human sorrow and conflict. The other wolf represents joy, love, generosity, and compassion, all the things that we associate with harmony and happiness and peace. So, the grandson thinks about all this for a while and asks, 'But which one wins?' And the grandfather answers, 'The one you feed.'"

Grace paused for a moment. I could tell she was remembering that day when her mother told her that story. Then she said, "It seems like the Choice Map is saying something similar. Like at any moment we can choose to feed Judger or choose to feed Learner."

Just as she said this, the alarm sounded on her phone. She always sets it to alert her when it's time to get ready for work. She glanced at her phone and checked her reminders.

"Oh, no! I nearly forgot about a meeting this morning. Ben, I'm so sorry. I'd love to call in late and continue this conversation, but I really need to scoot."

In the next instant, she was dashing up the stairs to finish getting ready, leaving me to ponder the two wolves, the Choice Map, and what it meant to feed Learner or Judger mindsets. Twenty minutes later she kissed me goodbye and raced out the door. When I got around to pouring myself another cup of coffee, I glanced at the refrigerator and realized the Choice Map was gone. Grace had taken it to work with her!

As I was getting in my car to leave for the office, I noticed a piece of paper stuck under the windshield wiper. It was a hurriedly written note from Grace:

Darling,

Thank you so much for the Choice Map—and especially for the good talk this morning. You can't imagine how much it means to me!

Love,
Grace

I felt great about the note, but I hadn't expected Grace to take the Choice Map. Clearly, she liked Joseph's ideas or she wouldn't have taken it. At least for now, I'd redeemed myself in her eyes. Good! That was one less pressure in my life.

CHAPTER 6

Switching Questions

"Everything can be taken from a man but one thing: the last of the human freedoms—to choose one's attitude in any set of circumstances, to choose one's own way."

Viktor E. Frankl

As I stepped off the elevator at the Pearl Building, I found Joseph watering his trees with a large red watering can. It surprised me to see him doing something I would have handed off to my staff. He turned to me with a friendly smile. "I love having plants around. It's a daily reminder that all living things require our attention," he said. "No office should be without at least a plant or two. My wife, Sarah, is the gardener in our family. She says being a good gardener requires you to ask good questions. Are your plants getting enough water, enough sun? Do they need a little pruning? Do they need nutrients? She says our plants thrive on good questions, just as we humans do."

Joseph quickly completed his gardening, and we went inside.

"When we finished our last meeting," he said, "we were discussing the Choice Map and what it tells us about Learner and Judger mindsets. Have you had any further thoughts about any of this?"

I guardedly told him about Grace, our talk in the kitchen,

and how she'd taken the Choice Map from the refrigerator. I even thought about telling him about the two wolves but decided it best to keep focused on his material.

"It's clear that we get different results depending on which of the two paths we take—Learner or Judger," I told Joseph hesitantly. "Maybe I get stuck in Judger more than I'd like to admit."

"Fortunately, there's a fast track out of Judger as soon as you recognize that Judger mindset has you in its grip." Joseph pointed to the little road in the middle of the map, joining the Judger and the Learner path. A sign labeled it the Switching Lane (see Figure 3). "That lane is the key to change. Once you notice you're in Judger—I mean non-judgmentally of course—you get to Learner by asking Switching questions. Let's look at how that works.

"When you're standing in Judger," Joseph continued, "the whole world usually looks pretty bleak. Even though the world is filled with infinite possibilities, we have only limited access to noticing them when seeing with Judger eyes or listening with Judger ears. Let me show you how to change your viewpoint, how to see and hear everything differently, sometimes almost immediately. For a moment, locate yourself on the Judger Path, right where the Switching Lane begins."

I turned my attention to the map and focused on the juncture of the Judger path and the Switching Lane.

"Any time you step onto this path," he continued, pointing to the Switching Lane, "you automatically step into choice. You wake up. You uncover a whole new view of the world. You literally switch how you're thinking about what's possible. When you observe your own thoughts, especially Judger ones, they relax their

Figure 3. The Switching Lane

grip on you, and you increase your freedom to choose what to think and do next.

"You seem to be talking about choice like it's an innate capacity."

"Absolutely! We're all born with that capacity," Joseph exclaimed. "That's what makes us human. We are always free to choose our mindset, though it takes practice, and sometimes courage. Bear in mind, the ability to choose doesn't mean we are in complete control of the outcome however much we might wish that. You may know about Viktor Frankl, who wrote *Man's Search for Meaning*. He spoke of 'the last of human freedoms—to choose one's attitude in any given circumstances, to choose one's own way.'"

I'd read Frankl's book in a college class and still had it on a bookshelf at home. Though I don't think I fully appreciated it at the time, the quote had stuck in my mind, especially realizing he'd written it as a prisoner in a Nazi concentration camp!

"Making this insight about the freedom to choose practical—and not just a bunch of fancy words—that's where the rubber hits the road," Joseph continued. "Keep in mind that as often as not your body tells you when you've jumped into Judger and we tend to respond automatically. Those signals from your body are quite straightforward, tension in your jaw, shoulders up around your ears, fingernails jabbing into your palms as you make a fist. Or maybe you detect a subtle twitch of a small muscle in your face. Or it's a feeling like wanting to jump in and correct something the other person has said. However you sense that you might be in Judger, pause, take a deep breath, knowing that even this pause, this deliberate breath, makes real changes in your body and brain. In this more relaxed state, you can get curious. You can ask yourself, Am I in Judger? Of course, the tricky part is that you have to ask that question nonjudgmentally! This is the time for getting out of your own way and seeing the big picture or being more inclusive in the way you're operating. Ask yourself Learner questions, starting with 'Am I in Judger?' If the answer is 'Yes, I am in Judger,' you are taking that first step onto the Switching Lane. Ask simple questions such as: 'Do I want to be in Judger? And where would I like to be? Is this what I want to feel or do?'"

"Is it really that easy?" I asked, still a little skeptical.

Joseph laughed. "It's not always easy, but it is simple. The Switching Lane takes you to the Learner path. You'll find a list of Switching questions in your Users Guide. That list is another of the tools in the QT system."

Joseph was gazing thoughtfully out the window. "Let me tell you a story that illustrates how Switching questions can make a huge difference in performance and results. It's a true story about my daughter Kelly, who's an avid and quite accomplished gymnast. In college, she was even training for a national championship competition.

"Here's what happened. During training Kelly would perform quite well most of the time, but only most of the time. Each time she missed her mark she'd get angry at herself. Sarah and I knew she'd never make the team that way. She had the ability, but her performance was too erratic. And her ability to recover from her mistakes was, let's say, under par.

"So, at her request, we worked with her using Question Thinking so she could make the improvement she needed to make the team. First, we asked what she thought about just before a performance. She discovered that in those crucial moments she always asked just one basic question, where am I going to mess up this time?"

"Which is a Judger question," I observed, thinking it was like something I'd say.

"Right," Joseph said, "because it focused her attention on falling and failing. Asking it led to what my daughter now calls Judger trouble. That question really interfered with her confidence and her performance. And it really created problems with her ability to recover from a mistake. So, the three of us worked on finding a Switching question she could ask herself to propel her quickly into Learner whenever she felt herself slipping into Judger. The new questions were Kelly's own ideas: How can I do a great job?

How can I do this beautifully and elegantly? That did the trick. Using those new questions, she reprogrammed herself by directing her attention in a positive direction. Her performance improved exponentially and became highly predictable. Kelly says that new question helps her stay in the zone."

"Did she make the team?"

"She sure did," Joseph said. "And, by the way, she came home with a trophy. It wasn't first place, but she was very pleased with herself, and so were her parents! I have to confess that 20 years ago, before I'd discovered how we can choose our mindsets, I would have probably chastised her for not taking first place and missed out on the joys of sharing my kids' struggles and victories. Oh, I tell you, having children teaches us to ask a whole new set of questions! By the way, you'll find Kelly's story in my Question Thinking Hall of Fame."

"This all sounds like a bit of magic, to me," I quipped. "Or even a miracle."

"Well, there's a time when I would have said that it's neither magic nor a miracle," Joseph replied, smiling. "I would have argued that It's mostly a method. But the years have taught me that maybe there's a little magic, too. Even, as you say, a miracle now and then! With questions we can even change ourselves physiologically. For example, the question, 'What if I get fired?' can set off a whole chain of biochemical stress reactions in your body. Kelly's question, 'Will I fall this time?' reminded her of past failures and made her anxious, which interfered with her performance and reinforced any old programming for failure. Consciously, of course, she didn't want to fail, but that's exactly what happened anyway with that old question. Learner questions program us with a positive intention—in Kelly's case, for the right attitude and optimal energy and coordination for an outstanding performance."

"By implication you're suggesting that Judgers can't be top performers," I reflected. "I can't agree with you there. I've known Judger types who were quite productive."

"I understand. But be careful about using labels like 'Judger types.' There isn't anybody who's a Judger person or a Learner person. These terms, as I use them, refer only to mindsets, and, as you know by now, every one of us has both mindsets, and always will. That's the conundrum of being human. Labels are just too handy, and that makes them sticky like self-adhesive stamps. Labeling other people has its own problems, such as causing them to back off, to be less engaged, and even, perhaps, unknowingly creating barriers with coworkers or friends or family members. And that can happen even if you think of them only as Judger types. As the saying goes, we pick up the vibes. On the other hand, our mindsets are dynamic. They change from moment to moment. The thing to remember, always, is that Question Thinking is about becoming aware of our mindsets, which puts us more in charge of making the changes we want.

"You are absolutely right that some people spend more time in Judger than Learner. And they may even be quite driven and productive. However, their successes often come with high costs in the form of unintended consequences. Such people can drive themselves and everyone around them crazy, alienating others or making them afraid of thinking on their own. Eventually that lowers productivity, cooperation, and creativity. Not to mention morale! It's hard to feel truly loyal to or trust someone who operates out of Judger most of the time. We may fear the consequences of not following them but that's not the kind of loyalty that draws the best from us. As often as not, it turns out to be divisive and in a large organization can result in costly turnover within what might otherwise have become an effective team.

"If you want people to be really engaged, resilient and involved, Learner is the path to take. An organization led by people in high Judger tends to have greater levels of stress, conflict, burnout, and more people problems. Those kinds of leaders are not well equipped to be flexible and adaptable—or successful—in meeting challenges. And just imagine the havoc that Judger plays when you take that mindset home with you at night!

"My wife, Sarah, once wrote an article exploring the difference between high Judger marriages and high Learner marriages. Her premise was that our experience of intimate relationships will be very different depending on whether we look on our partner with Learner eyes or Judger eyes. Sarah points out that with Learner eyes we're able to focus on what we appreciate about the other person and what's working in our relationship, at least most of the time. We build from strengths rather than dwelling on flaws–our own or our partner's."

I nodded. What his wife Sarah said made a lot of sense.

"When we're in Judger, whether at home or work, every difference of opinion can look like an insurmountable roadblock. We easily get into thinking there are only three options—fight, flee, or freeze. Or maybe hiding by going along because you don't want to rock the boat. But there is another option. We can go back to basic

Switching questions, like: Will being in Judger get me what I really want? Where would I rather be? What am I responsible for in this situation? Pause, take a deep breath. Put yourself on the Switching Lane and you can step right onto the Learner path."

"If what you say is true, I could just stay in Learner by always keeping those questions in mind."

"Theoretically, yes. But life isn't that simple. And not one of us is a saint. We're all going to fall into Judger from time to time—that's the point I'm emphasizing when I say we're all recovering Judgers," Joseph continued. "But I promise you this—the more you take to heart the Choice Map and Switching questions, the faster you'll be able to step into Learner, the easier it will be, and the longer you'll be able to stay there. You'll also spend less time in Judger and the experience will usually be less intense, so the consequences of being there will be minimized.

"And remember," Joseph continued, "Judger has two faces, one being judgmental toward ourselves, the other being judgmental toward others. The results can look quite different, but they come from that same judgmental, critical place in our thinking.

"If we focus our Judger mindset on ourselves, for example, with questions such as: Why am I such a failure? we hurt our self-confidence and may even feel depressed. On the other hand, when we focus our Judger mindset on others, with questions such as: Why is everyone around me so stupid and frustrating? we tend to get angry, resentful, and hostile. Either way, with Judger, we usually end up in conflict either with ourselves or with others. When Judger takes control it's impossible to find genuine connection, resolution, or any sense of peace. That's why many mediators use the Learner/Judger mindset material with their clients, especially the Choice Map. In conflict situations, there's a strong tendency to focus Judger on other people. Mediators know that the only the only way through such a conflict is by creating a level playing field where productive conversations become possible. And the fastest way to do this is with a Learner mindset. That's what makes productive conversations possible.

"Let me give you an example of Judger when we aim it at ourselves. Years ago, Sarah was talking with Ruth, her editor at one of the magazines she writes for. They were sharing how they had both had issues with managing their weight. Sarah told Ruth how she used the Choice Map to help her feel calmer, be kinder to herself, and make better choices about eating. Ruth got so excited that she asked Sarah to write an article about her experiences.

"In the article, Sarah described how the questions people typically ask themselves about eating either get them in trouble with their weight, self-image, and self-confidence or help them to be successful and satisfied with themselves. The troublemaker questions she listed included: What's wrong with me? Why am I out of control again? Why am I such a hopeless glutton?"

"Those are all judgmental questions," I interjected.

"Right. And whenever Sarah started down the Judger path with questions like those, she really beat herself up, which of course sent her spiraling right down to the Judger Pit. Unfortunately, those Judger meltdowns usually caused her to feel out of control and eat even more. Sometimes that led to real bingeing. Once Sarah recognized the impact those troublemaker Judger questions had on her, she decided to look for Switching questions to rescue herself. She said that Switching questions are the best thing she's ever found for getting back in control and feeling good about herself. Her new questions included: What's really going on with me? How do I want to feel? And am I willing to accept and forgive myself?

"Which got her onto the Switching Lane, her shortcut back to Learner," I said.

"Right again. Once she switched into Learner, she figured out some questions to help her stay there whenever she felt herself going Judger: What will serve me best right now? Am I being honest with myself? What do I really need? What can I do to feel better that doesn't involve eating? Whenever she asked herself one of these questions, she felt empowered rather than out of control. Not only that, but she's also gotten herself in great shape. She tells me it's pretty easy to maintain her weight now."

Judging by the photos of Sarah on Joseph's desk, I certainly didn't think Sarah looked like someone with weight issues. But all this talk was making me even more uncomfortably aware of how often the questions I asked myself were straight out of Judger mindset.

"From what I've seen so far," Joseph said, in a surprisingly accepting tone of voice, "while you obviously don't have trouble with your weight, you still have a lot of self-Judger going on."

"I can't disagree," I hedged. "But what's your basis for saying that?"

"That's easy," Joseph said. "Do you remember that time you were so sure I saw you as a Judger and a loser?"

"Yes," I said, hesitantly, sensing I was stepping into something I would regret.

"That's the perspective that keeps you bogged down and resigned about being able to change. But while you aim judgmental questions at yourself," Joseph said, looking straight at me, "you're also pretty good at targeting other people."

"I agree I can be pretty hard on myself...and on other people." I began to squirm. "But sometimes people really are jerks and idiots. I know I'm right about that. You've got to accept this as a fact of life and exercise good common sense, or good judgment, as you already said."

Without comment, Joseph directed my attention back to the Choice Map. As I held it in my hand, he leaned forward and pointed at the figure that was starting down the Judger Path. Then he pointed to the thought bubble over the figure's head. It contained just one question, which I read out loud: Whose fault is it?

What jumped into my mind were all the troubles I'd been having at work. I focused on that stark moment of truth when I concluded I was a failure and would have to resign. The shame I felt was just awful. Did Judger have a hand in shame, too? I was certainly in my Judger head at that moment, having judged myself as a loser. But wasn't I justified? I couldn't deny I'd screwed up.

"What's going through your mind right now?"

I replied with discomfort, "The more we talk, the more I see I've got to accept the blame for a lot of what's happened."

"Blame," Joseph said. "Tell me exactly what that word means to you."

"The bottom line? It means I should step down. I'm the incompetent one here. I'll never make it as a leader, no matter how badly I want it. Period! End of conversation."

"Hold on, Ben. Back up for a moment. Let's see what happens when you change your question from 'Who's to blame?' to 'What am I responsible for?'"

Joseph was right. Those questions did hit me differently, but I couldn't figure out why. "Blame. Responsibility. Aren't they the same thing?"

"Not at all," Joseph said. "Blame is Judger. Responsibility is Learner. There's a world of difference between them. Focusing on blame blinds us from seeing real alternatives and solutions. It's almost impossible to fix a problem when operating from Judger blame. Blame can be paralyzing. Blame keeps us stuck in the past. Responsibility, on the other hand, paves the path for a better future. If you focus your questions on what you might be responsible for, it gives you power and you also open your mind to new possibilities. You're free to create alternatives that lead to positive change."

Blame keeps us stuck in the past.
Responsibility paves the path for a better future.

Blame can be paralyzing. What did he mean by that? I felt an urge to get up, stretch, and walk around. I took a break, went to the bathroom, and splashed some cold water on my face. After I returned, Joseph said, "Remind me about what you said about Charles the other day."

Ah, back to Charles! Now I knew I was on solid ground. It would be easy to prove to Joseph how good judgment served me in this case, that my feelings about Charles were not just the product of Judger attitudes. "I told you, if it weren't for Charles, I wouldn't be in such a mess," I said. "That's obvious. He's playing a win-lose game. You'd have to be blind not to see that."

Without replying, Joseph directed me to turn to my Users Guide and find the charts labeled Learner/Judger Mindsets Learner/Judger Relationships (see Figures 4 and 5). I studied those pages for a moment, checking out the two columns that listed key characteristics of Learner and Judger. The content of those two columns was very different. It hit me immediately how

Learner/Judger Mindsets	
Judger Mindset	**Learner Mindset**
Judgmental (of self/others/facts)	Accepting (of self/others/facts)
Reactive and automatic	Responsive and thoughtful
Critical and negative	Appreciative and has humility
Close-minded	Open-minded
Know-it-all, self-righteous	Comfortable with not-knowing
Blame oriented	Responsibility oriented
Own point of view only	Takes multiple perspectives
Inflexible and rigid	Flexible/adaptive/creative
Either/or thinking	Both/and thinking
Defends assumptions	Questions assumptions
Mistakes are bad	Mistakes are to learn from
Presumes scarcity	Presumes sufficiency
Possibilities seen as limited	Possibilities seen as unlimited
Primary stance: protective & fearful	Primary stance: curious & open

Figure 4. Learner/Judger Mindset Chart
(Both mindsets are normal; each of us has both and always will. With awareness, each of us has the capacity to choose where we relate from in any moment.)

one way of thinking would take me down the Judger path while the other would pull me up to Learner territory.

"This chart guides us to become much better observers of ourselves." Joseph said. "It lists Learner and Judger qualities and characteristics to help us discern where we are at any moment. It's invaluable for helping us to strengthen our observer self and shift from Judger to Learner. Let's use it right now to do some exploring. Think about Charles. Then read off any words or phrases that leap to your attention."

I studied the pages. Reactive and automatic. Know-it-all.

Learner/Judger Relationships	
Judger Relating	**Learner Relating**
Win-lose relating	Win-win relating
Dismissive, demeaning	Accepting, empathizing
Advocacy	Inquiry
Separate from self/others	Connected with self/others
Fears differences	Values differences
Feedback considered rejection	Feedback considered worthwhile
Conversation: own agenda	Conversation: collaborative
Conflict perceived as destructive	Conflict considered constructive
"Judger ears" listen for:	"Learner ears" listen for:
Agree or disagree	Understanding and facts
What's wrong re: self and/or others	What's valuable re: self and/or others
Danger	Possibility
Seeks to attack or is defensive	Seeks to appreciate/resolve/create
Problem focused	Solution focused

Figure 5. Learner/Judger Relationship Chart
(Both mindsets are normal; each of us has both and always will. With awareness, each of us has the capacity to choose where we relate from in any moment.)

Listening for agreement or disagreement. Self-righteous... I stopped. Everything I was reading was in the Judger Mindset column. My jaw tightened. Then I turned to the Learner Mindset column. Only one phrase caught my eye: Comfortable with not-knowing. I was puzzled.

"I'm not sure what you mean by comfortable with not-knowing," I said.

"It's like when someone is doing research," Joseph explained. "You want to discover something new, which is impossible if you're attached to the conviction that you already know the answers. Valuing not-knowing is the basis of learning and all creativity and innovation. It's the state of mind that's open to all kinds of new possibilities and even hoping you might be surprised. Instead of defending old opinions or positions or answers, your goal is to look with fresh eyes. Remember Einstein's words: 'Learn from yesterday, live for today, hope for tomorrow. The important thing is to not stop questioning.' I like to think of this as 'rational humility,' a maturity we develop by admitting that it's impossible to ever have all the answers."

Rational humility! I liked that. That's how it felt when I was doing technological research. Beyond that, especially with relationships, I felt like I was in foreign territory.

Suddenly, I was confused. Was it Charles or me who was reactive and automatic? Was it Charles or me who was the know-it-all? Who was listening for agreement or disagreement? Who was self-righteous? Who was the big Judger here?

Before I could recover from my confusion, Joseph hit me with a new question. "What do you think it costs you to spend so much time in the Judger Pit?"

"Costs me?" I said quietly, looking at Joseph and then at the floor. His question had hit me like a thunderbolt. "I don't even want to think about the cost to the company for my Judger habits. First of all, I'm getting a good salary, but it's money down a black hole in terms of what I'm producing. On top of that, I'm starting to suspect that I've created a no-win situation that's brought my whole team down. I dread going to meetings with those people. And the trickle down to other departments we work with...well, this isn't a pretty picture!"

Joseph was nodding, apparently satisfied with my insights. "This is real progress," he told me. "You're doing great, Ben."

"What are you talking about? This is a disaster. Throw me a lifeline, would you? How do I get out of this?"

"I could drag you out," Joseph said, "but I'm going to give you something even more valuable—tools to get yourself out. I'm a big believer in the 'teach 'em to fish' philosophy. Now, I want you to bring to mind a time when you were in Learner in a work situation. Got the picture? Recall as vividly as you can what that experience was like. If you have trouble remembering, look at the Learner side of the chart."

Right away I recalled my best work at KB Corp, how everything flowed, how I woke up every morning looking forward to going to work. My productivity was high. So was everybody else's. We were all really engaged. People even said they enjoyed working with me, though the truth is I spent a lot of time alone. I could feel myself smiling at the memory. My work life then couldn't have been any more different from the nightmare I was experiencing now.

"I just had a thought," I said. "At KB I didn't have to deal with people much except to come up with innovative answers to their technological questions. Under those circumstances, it wasn't such a challenge to stay in Learner."

"I see what you mean," Joseph said. "Applying those same principles to your present leadership role might be a challenge. Humans aren't machines."

"That's what my wife keeps telling me," I said.

We both chuckled.

"So, let me see if I understand you correctly," Joseph said. "With technology problems, your Learner curiosity is natural and easy. You're very good at that. You have specific questions that help you to step outside yourself to make objective observations, to test your assumptions, and assess what's going on. In those situations, you understand that whatever you come up with is neither good nor bad—it's simply information. Thomas Edison was famous for telling people how it took thousands of failures to invent the electric light bulb and that each failure contributed to that final successful solution.

"I'm giving you new tools to take advantage of what you already know how to do. When you can recognize Judger, distinguish it from Learner, and switch to Learner whenever you choose, that's self-coaching. And you're well on your way to taking charge of your life—at work and at home."

Suddenly something clicked for me. I turned my attention

to the Choice Map as Joseph spoke and focused on the Switching Lane. "Switching is what makes it possible to change," I exclaimed. "That's where the action is!"

> Switching is what makes it possible to change.
> That's where the action is!

Joseph nodded emphatically. "Yes! You've got it!" he exclaimed. "The ability to switch puts you in charge of change. Being able to nonjudgmentally observe your own Judger and then ask a Switching question—well, that's about the most powerful and courageous thing anybody can do for themselves. It's the operational heart of change, what many people call self-management or self-regulation. Combining the willingness and the ability to switch leads not only to change, but it also makes us able to sustain change, because we're observing and asking ourselves Learner questions moment by moment by moment."

Joseph's enthusiasm was contagious.

"Let me check this out," I said, a bit nervous that I might be putting my own spin on it. "What I hear you saying is that the same hot buttons that normally trigger our natural fight-or-flight reactions can be understood in a different way. We can learn to read them as signals that we're in Judger. And this ability gives us the opportunity to reach for a Switching question to get us on the Learner path."

"Exactly," Joseph said. "Exactly!"

I was eager to learn more, especially the parts about change and sustaining change and how that could improve my results at work. But a glance at the clock told me that today's meeting was coming to an end.

CHAPTER 7

Switching Strategies, Body and Mind

"Taking responsibility for your beliefs and judgements gives you the power to change them."

Byron Katie

As I was leaving the office for my next meeting with Joseph, I nearly collided with Charles in the hallway. It happened so fast I was caught off-guard. He'd burst from his office with a handful of papers, looking harried and annoyed. I'd managed to mumble a half-hearted good morning, just to be cordial, but instead of returning my greeting, he shook his handful of papers practically in my face.

"It was a good morning until these landed on my desk!" he said, turning on his heel and darting off, leaving me standing there speechless.

I went into a slow burn, fueled by the adrenalin that screeched through my body and brain. The near collision with Charles combined with his rude behavior, brought up every issue I'd ever had with him. My shoulders tightened, my stomach knotted up, and my fingers curled into fists. Tight fists! Whoa, I told myself. As startling and aggravating as our near collision had been, did it warrant this reaction? If Joseph was right, all these discomforts and stresses I was experiencing were symptoms of my mindset going Judger.

Frankly, I was more than a little disappointed with myself. I thought I had been doing a pretty good job of recognizing when I was slipping into Judger and asking the kinds of questions that would take me to the Switching Lane. But here I was with Judger sensations coursing through every cell of my body and brain. My heart pounded and every breath felt like an effort. Even finding the Switching Lane at that moment seemed about as likely as climbing Mount Everest. Moreover, my Judger mindset was yelling at me that everything I was experiencing was real and justified and sometimes you just had to face that fact. Like it or not, something had to be done about Charles.

By the time I got to Joseph's office, my neck was so cramped up it felt like a steel rod had been inserted. My mind raced a mile a minute, fueled by that near-miss in the hallway and every other aggravating encounter I'd ever had with Charles. I was even obsessing about all the things I should have said. And, of course, I was rehearsing the talk I was going to have with him to set things straight once and for all. The message was clear: this guy had to go. Was I going to have to talk to Joseph about this?

As I pulled the door open to the building where Joseph had his office, I felt like turning around, going home, and starting the day all over again. Was I making too much of this encounter with Charles? I didn't think so. But if that was true, why did I feel I was letting Joseph down by failing to handle things better after all the hours he'd spent coaching me? At this rate I certainly wasn't turning out to be his star student. I feared I could be turning into his worst embarrassment!

When I arrived at Joseph's office, I found him standing in the foyer as if he'd been waiting for me. "What happened to you?" he asked, stepping back. "You look like you're on the verge of punching somebody out."

I shrugged, embarrassed he was seeing me like this, wallowing around in the Judger Pit. I began rubbing my neck to ease my tension. "I'm okay," I said. "I just had an unfortunate encounter with Charles. I thought I'd made some progress with him but now I'm thinking it's a lost cause."

Joseph raised an eyebrow like he was more than a little concerned. "No broken bones, I hope," he said, with a smile. "No blood spilled?"

"Nothing like that," I said.

He gestured for me to follow him to his inner office.

"Maybe I should unwind a bit before we talk," I said as we prepared to sit down.

"I have an idea," he said, "Stay with what you're feeling. It might be a good opportunity to take a closer look at what happens in your body and brain when Judger mindset takes charge. Knowing our inner workings can give us a head start on the Switching Lane."

I felt like the proverbial deer in headlights, unsure where he was going with all this. It was my responsibility to deal with Charles, not his. Wasn't it? Didn't I have to be the one who decided when Judger was justified? Joseph was silent, waiting for me to make the next move. After a few seconds, I shrugged. His confident demeanor told me it might be worthwhile to follow his lead.

"I hope this isn't going to be one of those touchy-feely exercises," I said, only half joking.

He smiled. "Consider it personal research," he said. "In fact, there's a bit of science involved. Let's start with you describing what's going on with you…without thinking too hard about it."

"That's easy. I'm feeling a little stupid," I blurted out. "Angry and embarrassed for getting bogged down in Judger. I've got to have a showdown with Charles to clear the air. But in my present state of mind…well, I'd probably make a Judger mess of it."

"The two faces of Judger," he said. "Remember when we discussed that?"

It took me a second to recall. "Yes. There's Judger toward ourselves and Judger toward others."

Joseph nodded. "And you've got both going on at once." He got that look on his face as if a light bulb had lit up in his head. "I just remembered something." He stepped over to his desk, opened a drawer, reached in, and came back to me with what looked like a blank business card. Curious, I took it from his hand and turned it over. On the other side, in bold letters, it read. "Don't believe everything you think!"

I started to read it aloud, then paused. "Don't believe everything I think? If I don't believe everything I think, what or whom can I believe?"

"Keep asking yourself questions just like that. And change your questions often!"

"Wait," I said. "I've got this. I remember what you said at our last meeting. You said instead of asking why am I such a failure, or who's to blame, ask what am I responsible for?"

"Good start!" Joseph said. After a minute or so, he asked, "What's happening with you now?"

I was pretty sure he was referring to the look of surprise on my face. "A minute ago, that Switching Lane had dropped right off my radar," I said. "Now it's right in front of me, just a breath away."

"Okay," Joseph said. "Step right up and take that path. Now tell me, do you notice any changes in how your body feels?"

"My body? What does my body have to do with it?"

Joseph was silent, waiting for my response.

"Oh, I see," I answered. "Or should I say I feel?" There could be no doubt about it. My neck no longer felt like it had a steel rod inserted. My back was more relaxed. And those cramps I'd been feeling in my belly were fading away. I was relaxing. "How can a simple question change all that?" Frankly, I wasn't sure I believed what my own body was telling me.

"What are you thinking about Charles right now? Any changes there?"

"Charles! Did you have to remind me about him? And, uh, didn't you promise me something about a science lesson?"

Joseph laughed. "Okay, here's your science. We'll get back to Charles later. Step one is that you already experienced the most important part of the lesson."

"What did I experience? When did I do that?"

Joseph seemed to be considering his answer carefully. Then he said, "You experienced it when you and Charles nearly collided in the hallway."

"But everything happened so fast… I started to argue that there wasn't any science in that. But I shut up before finishing my thought. All I could remember was getting startled and almost lashing out at Charles.

Joseph drew a small pointer device from his pocket and clicked on a monitor across the room. Suddenly we were looking at a cutaway graphic of the human brain. He focused his laser pointer on two almond sized shapes near the center of the brain.

"Okay," Joseph said. "Here's your science lesson. These two little masses of neurons, the amygdala, hold the secret of what happens in our bodies and brains whenever we perceive a threat to our well-being. This can be anything from having a close call in traffic, to the pressure of a tight deadline, to having an argument with an important person in our life."

"Or like a certain person we won't name nearly knocking me down?"

"That, too," Joseph said, nodding. He continued his lesson in a teacherly tone. "Brain scientists tell us that the amygdala is our first line of defense, alerting us to danger. We wouldn't be here today without our amygdala."

"I remember my biology," I said. "The amygdala is the alarm system that sets off our basic survival mechanism. Fight or flight. Right?"

Joseph nodded. "Right. I'd like to elaborate a bit, however. Our first response to danger might be to hide. That failing, we'd better be ready to fight or run for our lives. Failing that, we're likely to freeze and offer ourselves up as lunch for the proverbial Saber-Toothed tiger. But from the neurosciences we learn it's more complicated than this. The tiny amygdalae interact with many other systems of our bodies and brains."

"Like telling our legs to start running or our fists to start flying."

"There's much more that happens before that," Joseph said. "Let's back up a bit, to the nanosecond when the amygdala first receives signals from the senses—a loud noise, a bad smell, the snap of a twig…"

"Or someone bursting from a doorway…"

Joseph chuckled. "That, too," he said. "Here's where things get complicated. And it all happens at the speed of light. The amygdala, we believe, starts off the processing of information from our senses, our memories of past emotional or physical traumas, even information about the readiness of our big muscles to launch our physical defense. It also sets off the production of biochemicals in our brains and bodies, changing functions such as heart rate, blood flow, adrenal function, alertness, and aggressiveness, even sharpening our senses. And it's at this point that our brain gets to work interpreting all this information and how to respond. We do our best to make sense of what's going on, and then decide, for better or for worse, what we're going to do about it. All this happens in nanoseconds. From this collection of information our brains interpret what all of this means, and we put together stories to guide our actions.

"One of my favorite scientists, Dr. Candace Pert, puts it this way: 'we all make up stories to describe so-called reality when incoming information hits our higher brain. And of course, we all get to create our own version of what's going on.'"

"That's it? We create stories?"

"Keep in mind that our brains organize and direct all movement in our lives." Joseph paused and thought. "Let me share a story with you. When I was a young man, my uncle introduced me to the martial arts. I was kind of a fearful kid. He thought a few Karate moves would toughen me up to face the world. I did learn a few moves. But that wasn't what made me less fearful. Martial arts helped me become more fully aware of my fears, even make friends with them. In doing so, I learned I could better choose my responses to what I'd once perceived as threatening situations. I was no longer limited to reacting automatically."

"Hard to imagine you as a scared little kid," I said.

"Oh, yes. It's true. I'd freeze up or try to get away whenever I felt threatened. We never get very far in life if running or freezing, or even fighting, are our main responses. I like to think that Question Thinking was born that summer at the Karate dojo. It was there that I discovered choice. I learned to ask myself, am I focusing on what didn't work or on finding something that does? In terms of Question Thinking, you might say this was my first baby step of intentionally moving from Judger to Learner. Each time I took that journey, and really paid attention, I gave my brain opportunities for change, for making new choices. To quote our friend Dr. Pert again, we all have the 'ability to either blame others or take responsibility for our actions.' That's where the Choice Map comes in. It provides us with the guidance for creating the stories we tell ourselves about what's going on."

"Are you trying to tell me how to earn a black belt in Question Thinking," I suggested.

"That's one way of putting it," Joseph said, "Brain scientists talk about neuroplasticity, that is, the brain's potential for creating new neuropathways, and thus new ways to interact with the world. That includes pathways associated with the amygdala. Therein lies the secret of how we change our responses to danger. Getting back to you and Charles. I assure you that your feelings about him are real. Your challenge lies in your interpretation of those feelings and the questions you ask about them. Where do the stories about that encounter come from, and where are they going to take you? Remember, your reaction to that near-collision in the hall was triggered by your amygdala activating memories and stories created in the past. And if fear was any part of those past stories, you can count on your automatic response to be negatively biased—throwing you right into Judger."

I thought about this for a moment. "If what you say is true, I wasn't just highjacked by Judger, I was ambushed by my amygdala!"

Joseph nearly cracked up laughing. But I was serious. I really did feel like I'd been ambushed. It was an ambush coming from inside my own body and brain. And it was very unsettling to think that I might have no control of this reaction. Or did I?

"I'm like a puppet on a string," I said, feeling discouraged. "And my amygdala is the puppet master."

"It can seem so at times," Joseph said consolingly. "But here's what actually happens in your brain. Almost in the same nanosecond that it is stimulated, your amygdala accesses your memories of past experiences when you felt frightened or were in danger. Or when you were actually injured or traumatized. Or when you've witnessed someone close to you injured. That's the information we access when we sense danger. You can't erase these old memories, but you can minimize their influence by providing your amygdala with new information for responding in more appropriate and effective ways."

"How do we do that? By waving a magic wand?"

"Wouldn't that be nice? But no. Your new information, and thus your new strategies start with learning new ways to interpret the very early signals from your amygdala."

"I'd have to be a fortune teller and see into the future."

"It's much simpler than that, "Joseph said. "The first information you need is right there in your body. You can feel it. Remember what you were experiencing when we started this session, what your research told you?"

"You mean like feeling my heart beating faster, and breathing harder, different muscles tensing up...fingers coiling into fists."

"Exactly. And if your brain-mouth connection is too well lubricated at that moment, you blurt out something you later regret."

"And it's too late by then."

"That's right," Joseph said. "But you learn how to catch yourself earlier and earlier as you go along, with the first sensations of your body being nudged into action. Many famous writers, including Victor Frankl, Rollo May, and Stephen Covey, have spoken of our capacity to be aware of the gap between stimulus and response. That means between what happens and what you do about it. It is here, in this gap, this inner space, that we find our greatest freedom...our freedom to choose and, as Rollo May put it, 'to use this gap constructively.' But how do we do that?"

"You're suggesting that Question Thinking…the Choice Map…" I became tongue-tied and couldn't finish what I had started to say. Joseph filled in the blanks for me.

"By employing these tools I call Question Thinking," he said, "we can provide our amygdala with new information for interpreting the stimulus, for asking new questions and opening our minds to possibilities beyond running or fighting or hiding."

"Or freezing up," I added.

Joseph nodded. "In the world we live in, there's often a lot riding on our ability to take advantage of that space, that all-important gap, between stimulus and response. By putting the amygdala under their microscope and unveiling its inner workings, neuroscience has made it much easier to inhabit this important space in our minds. This gap is where we can pause, step back, ask different questions, and create different stories, different ways of interpreting what we've just experienced. And in the process, we can choose what we do next."

"Sort of like learning it was okay to sail our ships beyond the horizon," I said.

"Beg your pardon?" Joseph asked, puzzled by my remark.

"You know," I said. "We first had to be convinced that the world wasn't flat."

"Very funny," Joseph said, shaking his head with a big grin on his face. "But not a bad analogy. The first stories we told about the earth was that it was flat and we'd sail off the edge of the earth when we reached the horizon. But sailors had new experiences from which they created new stories about the shape of the earth. And that, in turn, gave us a whole new world of choices and opportunities."

I had to gather my thoughts and try to process all that Joseph had been saying. Thankfully, at this moment my cell phone buzzed. I automatically reached into my pocket to fish it out. This was a good excuse for taking a needed break. I glanced at Joseph. "I better pick this up."

He nodded. "That's fine. We can resume when you're done."

I was relieved when Joseph got up and left the room so I'd have some privacy. I checked the caller ID on my phone, hoping it was Grace. It wasn't. It was Charles! The last person I wanted to speak with right now. But I pressed the green phone icon and said hello.

"Hey, Ben," Charles said. To my surprise, his voice was light and cheerful. "Just checking in with you. Sorry for my abruptness this morning. You must have thought I'd lost my mind. I nearly did, to tell the truth. There was a major mix-up on a job order that would have been a disaster for us. But I'm happy to say the problem is solved. I'll fill in the details at our meeting this afternoon."

For a moment I was speechless. Charles apologizing! Was I hearing right? "Uh, that's fine…later is fine, Charles. I'm rather busy right now."

"Okay, then," Charles said. "Sorry for the interruption."

"Not a problem," I said. "Glad you called."

It took me a moment to recover from Charles' surprise call. And it made me start questioning my interpretation of what I'd felt and how I'd acted after our near collision. Back in the hall, I'd created a very different story around that experience than I was seeing now. I shuddered to think what would have happened if I had acted on my first story as if it were the absolute truth. When

Joseph returned, part of me was reluctant to tell him what had just happened. Then I decided I would, curious what his take on it would be.

"It's all a bit embarrassing, "I said. "I can't deny that when all that happened with Charles this morning, my mind went with the worst-case scenario—that negative bias thing you talk about with the amygdala—and created a story that could have been disastrous if I'd acted on it. Suddenly I see very different possibilities."

"Congratulations," Joseph said. "That negative bias, and the stories we create around it, is your fast track to Judger, plain and simple. Don't be embarrassed about that. Congratulate yourself for recognizing Judger and stepping onto the Switching Lane. And for recognizing the story you'd created." He paused, then added, smiling, "Happily, you had the good sense not to rearrange Charles' face along the way."

I almost jumped out of my seat. "I hope you don't think..."

"That you're capable of violence or actions that are anything but constructive? No more or less than any of us. But let me ask you something. If you were to relive that same encounter with Charles, would you be able to pause and find that space Frankl speaks of? Could you recognize Judger and switch to Learner?"

I nodded. "I'm pretty sure I could. The way you've laid it out really helps. By now, that Choice Map of yours is clearly imprinted in my brain. I can easily follow the process in my mind."

"Every time you are able to recognize the questions you're asking yourself, and the stories that go along with them, you have the opportunity to change them. You succeed in switching from Judger to Learner by providing new information to create a more accurate story of the events around you. This is the leading edge of your effectiveness as a human being." Joseph said. "Neuroscience has opened up a whole world of new possibilities for all of us."

"So, if my brain can do all you say…well, the Switching Lane is never more than a breath away. I have the capacity for strengthening and expanding my own built-in switching strategies."

Joseph paused. Then he grinned and said, "Ben, I think you're right. That's a great way to say it."

That felt really good, and I asked shyly, "Does that mean there's always hope that we can change even if at first it doesn't seem possible?"

His nod and smile said it all.

"The Choice Map gives us the ability to recognize our stories for what they are, to develop critical thinking around what they mean and where they are likely to take us. Pert called this ability selective attention, an ability to consciously shift our focus. If we focus our attention on Learner, we open our minds to new possibilities. If we focus our attention on Judger, we're sure to encounter conflict…"

"And close ourselves to new possibilities," I added.

"Right," Joseph said. "More often than not, the questions we ask ourselves and the stories we tell ourselves in Judger, are wrapped in blame and worse case scenarios, blocking any possibility for change."

We were both silent for several moments, my brain filled with the implications of our conversation.

"I can't help but add one more thing," Joseph said. He pointed to what at first looked like a framed letter hanging on the wall.

He went over and read it to me. "It's another quote from Candace Pert," he said. "'If we're so powerful, I also wonder what we want to create for this human existence, this planet of six billion people hurtling through space? It really is the next question to ponder.'"

CHAPTER 8

See with New Eyes, Hear with New Ears

"Authentic listening is not easy. We hear the words, but rarely do we really slow down to listen and to squint with our ears, to hear the emotions, fears, and underlying concerns."

Kevin Cashman

We started our next meeting with a question that had been bothering me since early in my conversations with Joseph. "Maybe it's just wishful thinking," I began, "but given the problems Judger throws our way…"

Joseph lifted his hand, signaling me to stop, and replied, "Remember, none of us can avoid slipping into Judger from time to time. It's only human. And part of the struggle we have with our humanness derives from our amygdala, as we've discussed." He smiled. "But you can free yourself from Judger by simply accepting that part of yourself. It helps, of course, to understand that the amygdala's responses can change with the new information we provide with Question Thinking. Judger is not the problem; it's how we relate to Judger that makes all the difference. It's such a simple formula: Judger-Switch-Learner. But nobody can make it work without beginning with acceptance."

"Huh? That doesn't make sense. How can I be free of something that's part of me?"

"It does sound like a contradiction, doesn't it," Joseph said. "But it is possible. Simple acceptance creates a level playing field where change becomes possible. As the famous psychologist Carl Jung said, 'We cannot change anything until we accept it.' But leveling the playing field can also be challenging, especially if Judger whispers in your ear a lot. Did Alexa ever tell you about her husband Stan's breakthrough?"

"She mentioned it," I replied. "You helped him to make a pile of money, as I understand it."

"He's very proud of that story," Joseph said. "He used the QT tools to earn his way into my Hall of Fame. Stan, as Alexa may have told you, is in the investment business. Accepting his own Judger turned out to be very profitable for him!

"Some years back, Stan was a very judgmental guy and very stuck in needing to be right. He didn't think of himself that way, but many people around him did. If he had a run-in with someone, or heard gossip about that person that wasn't flattering, he'd just write that person off. Stan will tell you that he clung to his assumptions and opinions like a bull terrier to a bone. He turned down many business opportunities on the basis of rumor, idle gossip, and guilt by association. He justified it all as a way of minimizing risk—which was only partially true.

"One time he made a very large investment in a promising startup. About a year later, the company hired a CEO who'd been employed by a firm that was implicated in a big financial scandal. This really pushed Stan's buttons. Although this new guy had been freed of any wrongdoing, Stan was caught up in the assumption that where there was smoke there was fire. He was on the verge of pulling out his money—at a huge loss to him, by the way. To put it mildly, he was in a great deal of conflict about the whole thing. Except for the CEO they'd hired, the company seemed to be doing everything right.

"About this time, Sarah and I had dinner with Stan and Alexa, and we were discussing the Learner/Judger material. Alexa brought up Stan's investment dilemma and encouraged him to question his assumptions and use Switching questions to evaluate his decision. She suggested he apply the ABCD Choice Process to that issue, one of the tools I've been promising to tell you about. At first Stan was resistant but then he agreed to try it. In the end he was amazed at what a big difference it made. Here's how the ABCD Choice Process works." Joseph flicked on the monitor across the room and the following chart came up (see Figure 6):

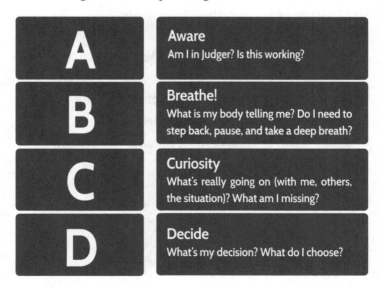

Figure 6. ABCD Choice Process

He gave me a moment to familiarize myself with the content before going on with his story. Then he labeled each step like it was a chapter and delineated each step.

"A—Aware! Am I in Judger? Stan was very funny about this. After we went over the characteristics of Judger, he amazingly admitted that an awful lot of what we described applied to him. His response surprised us: 'Being in Judger is my forte!' We all laughed, though we knew he was beginning to look at his behavior more honestly.

"B—Breathe! Do I need to pause, step back, take a deep breath and look at this situation more objectively? Stan smiled at this question, actually did take a deep breath, paused, and shortly admitted that he was being anything but objective, especially because so much money was at stake. He really distrusted this new CEO, though he'd never even spoken with the man.

"C—Curiosity. What's really going on here? What are the facts? What am I missing or avoiding? We asked Stan if he'd done anything to collect objective information. Did he have everything he needed to make a responsible judgment? Stan realized that he'd never gotten past his distaste for what he'd heard about this new hire at the startup. But facts? No, he admitted that he had no facts. That was a real eye opener for him.

"D—Decide. What's my decision? What's my choice? Well, by then Stan realized that he didn't have all the information he needed to make a wise choice. And because of his large investment he owed it to himself to check things out. A month later Stan called to tell me he'd checked around and found out the new CEO was a good guy who'd gotten caught up in someone else's mess. It was Stan's awareness and acceptance of Judger that allowed him to scrutinize his assumptions and open his mind about the new CEO. Long story short, Stan left his money in, the company went public two years later, and he made a fortune.

"The whole situation made Stan stop and think. It was a real wake-up call for him. Having realized how much money his Judger almost cost him, Stan tells me he now uses ABCD all the time. It's become an integral part of self-coaching for him. He even jokes that he's starting to hardwire those questions into his brain! None of this would have happened if he hadn't been able to simply observe and accept the Judger part of himself instead of pushing it away. Using the ABCD process begins with awareness and acceptance, then builds on it. Stan certainly reaped the rewards!

"If you met Stan today, you'd still notice that he can be opinionated and judgmental. He knows that part of himself very well and accepts it, but now he doesn't allow it to blind him in making decisions. He even has a sense of humor about his Judger. He said the ABCD process had shown him how to avoid committing assumacide. You know, death by assumption."

"Great story!" I said, and I really meant it, though I admit it took me a second to get what he meant by that word assumacide. If I hadn't shot myself in the head with my assumptions, I certainly had shot myself in the foot a few times! I found the ABCD formula in my Users Guide and jotted down a few notes.

"Think about Stan making all that money and my wife finally being successful with her weight," Joseph noted. "If they had continued wasting time being judgmental about their own Judger, and assuming that their judgements were right, they wouldn't have even gotten to first base in making the changes they wanted."

"This all sounds great," I said. "It really does. But here's something that still bothers me. Learner can sound soft…like you're just a beginner. How does this fit with the perception of good leaders having to be strong, tough, and decisive? How does being more of a Learner help me with that?"

"How about Alexa," Joseph countered. "How does she handle the tough calls?"

"Point made," I responded quickly, thinking back to some difficult decisions she had made that I wouldn't have wanted to face myself. She could be hard as nails when the situation demanded it, yet everyone who worked for her still felt respected even when she challenged us.

Joseph continued, "There's an important difference between 'Learner tough' and 'Judger tough.' You can get the job done from either position. However, a Learner leader displays the kind of toughness that builds trust, loyalty, and respect as well as cooperation and risk-taking. Judger leaders are more likely to generate fear, mistrust, and conflict in the people around them. That might not cost so much in the short-term but in the long-term it almost certainly will."

Was Joseph referring to my leadership style and nightmare team? Rather than bringing that up, I challenged him about something else that bothered me about Learner.

"Doesn't Learner slow things down?" I blurted out. "Work is just one pressure and deadline after another. Sometimes I'm staggered by the number of things I need to get done and how fast they must happen. If I had to be in Learner all the time, wouldn't it take forever to get anything done? I mean, wouldn't I end up more behind than ever?"

Joseph answered my question with more of his own. "How many times, when you were in a rush, have you made a mistake, blamed yourself or others, and then had to do it all over? How much extra time did that take? In your haste, how many times have you been impatient or impolite to someone and then noticed that he or she didn't talk to you much after that? What's the cost in time, results, and even loyalty when you treat people like that?"

I just stared at him. It felt like he had been watching me in my office all day long, five days a week. Then he added, "That's what happens when Judger takes over at work. On the other hand, I've heard over and over, from the folks in my Question Thinking Hall of Fame, that Learner truly helps them save time and increase productivity. In fact, one of them commented that speed and efficiency are not at all the same thing. Then he joked that Judger puts speed bumps in the path of efficiency and effectiveness!

"Judger makes speed bumps. I like that," I said. "It sure seems like life would be a lot simpler if we could all just recognize and accept Judger in ourselves, switch to Learner, and operate from there."

"How true!" Joseph said. "That's one of the ultimate goals of Question Thinking and what I like to call Learner Living. Imagine what work would be like if people did this most of the time. You would have a Learner culture; you could even say you have a Learner organization. And what about your team, Ben? The one you complain about so much. Are they in Judger or Learner most of the time? You know that teams and even organizations follow the mood and behavior of their leaders. As the leader of the team, your results will only get better if theirs do." He paused for a moment, then added: "Think of what we've been discussing as a practice, in the way that some people practice yoga, or mindfulness, or meditation. It's something you give quality attention to daily, sometimes hour by hour, sometimes moment by moment. You get better at it the more you practice. As one of my clients put it, this practice rewired his brain. I think it's true. Soon you'll see with new eyes and hear with new ears."

Joseph glanced at his watch. "We've been talking quite a while. We can take a short break and then go onto the next step, or we can wait until the next time we get together. What do you want to do?"

I was torn. I needed time to digest what we'd covered so far. But frankly, I was eager to hear the rest of what Joseph would tell me. I knew it would help with the conversation that would soon be coming up with Charles—and also with Grace. It took only a second to make my decision. "Okay, let's go for it!"

CHAPTER 9

Learner Teams and Judger Teams

"It's not differences that divide us.
It's our judgments about each other that do."

Margaret J. Wheatley

During our break, I started remembering what it had been like to work at KB. It had been very different from what I was now experiencing at QTec. When I compared the two experiences, there wasn't a doubt in my mind that at KB I had mostly been in Learner. As a research engineer and head tech guy, I did most of my work alone, then reported my findings to the team, taking their questions and providing answers. It was easy to be in Learner most of the time. By contrast, at QTec it was apparent that I was in Judger more often than I cared to admit. No matter where I looked, especially with my team, something seemed to be going wrong or somebody was failing to do what they were supposed to. How could I avoid going into Judger? As Joseph and I continued our meeting that day, I hesitantly shared this observation with him and said, "I'm not sure where to take it from here."

"I think I can best respond to that with a folk tale," Joseph replied. "You've probably heard of the mythologist Joseph

Campbell. He was famous for coming up with exactly the right story for every situation. Here's one I heard many years ago.

"It seems a farmer was out working his field when his plow caught on something, and it wouldn't budge. The horse reared up and the farmer cursed. After calming the horse, the farmer yanked back on the braces. But the plow still wouldn't budge. Because he was an impatient man his first reaction was to go Judger. Had a rock or other obstacle broken his plowshare? That could mean losing at least two days' work while he hauled the broken parts to the blacksmith! Cursing, he began digging around to free the plow. To his surprise, he discovered that it was caught on an iron ring buried six inches under the ground.

"After freeing his plow, the farmer got curious. He cleared away some of the dirt and pulled on the iron ring. Off came the lid of an ancient chest. He peeked down inside it. Before him, glittering in the sun, lay a treasure of precious jewels and gold.

"This story reminds us that it is often by confronting our toughest obstacles that we find our greatest strengths and possibilities, but sometimes we've got to dig deep to find them. Campbell had a phrase for it: Where you stumble, there lies your treasure. To uncover that treasure you'd ask yourself questions like: What could I discover? What haven't I noticed before? What might be valuable here?"

"Where you stumble, there lies your treasure."
Joseph Campbell

"That might be fine and well. But I'm still not seeing how all this is going to help me. Where's the treasure in this mess of mine?"

Joseph easily took up my challenge. "How about doing a little excavating," he said. "To start with, let's look at how your mindsets and your questions affect people around you." He leaned back in his chair and took a deep breath." For example, what about that team you're heading up? How often are you in Judger when you meet with them?"

"Truthfully? Just about every meeting lately!"

"And how would you say you communicate with the members of your team?"

"Communicate? That's a laugh! Listen, I told you how awful our meetings are. When I do call a meeting, nobody has much to offer. They sit on their hands and wait for me to tell them what to do. Finally, I talk, and Charles barrages me with his interminable questions. Doesn't matter what I say, he questions everything."

"Think of yourself as the farmer in Campbell's story," Joseph continued. "When you're with your team, are you cursing the fact that your plow got stuck, or are you getting curious about finding the door to the treasure? Are you looking for who's to blame or are you looking for what's working and what might be possible? Are you asking yourself questions like: How can I show them I have the right answer? Or are you asking: What can we discover and accomplish together? What could they contribute that I haven't thought of yet?"

I wasn't sure what I did, but I knew it wasn't what Joseph was suggesting. "I guess you'll have to clue me in here."

"Okay. You've been in conferences with Alexa, both in-person and by Zoom. How does she conduct her meetings? What does she say and do? How do her meetings affect you?"

"I look forward to Alexa's meetings," I told Joseph. "They're always enlivening. I feel like jumping right in, participating in any way I can. I come away with new ideas to pursue. But I've never been able to figure out what she does to generate that kind of energy and excitement."

The moment those words were out of my mouth, it hit me. "Alexa asks questions," I said. "Her meetings are all about questions. But not interrogating kinds of questions. She really piques everyone's interest and curiosity. Her questions are Learner ones, and they motivate us, sometimes even inspire us to participate in new ways."

Joseph sat back in his chair a moment before leaning forward enthusiastically. "Alexa's questions motivate you to contribute your best. She inspires people to abandon Judger and operate from Learner. That's the key to high engagement from your whole team. She likes to say that 'Learner begets Learner. And Judger begets Judger.' You could even call Alexa a Learner leader." Joseph paused for a moment and then asked, "How do you think her questions are different from yours? What experience do you want to create in your meetings moment by moment?"

Learner begets Learner.
And Judger begets Judger.

"Alexa has her style, I have mine," I said, getting a little defensive. "Do you ask questions?"

"Sure, I ask questions. Besides talking to my people in person, I send out emails and texts asking what they've accomplished. Or what they haven't accomplished, which is more to the point lately. I get very few replies, which is pretty maddening."

"When they do answer, how do you listen? How do you respond?"

"It depends. If the answer is any good, I might jot it down. But lately, I leave those meetings with nothing."

"Describe what the experience of listening is like for you," Joseph said.

That wasn't difficult. "Mostly I've been pretty annoyed and impatient," I replied, "especially when a person's answer doesn't come close to solving the problem, or when it shows that person is not following my plan. I get the impression nobody really cares."

"In situations like those, what's your attitude toward your colleagues? Are you in Learner or Judger most of the time?"

"What else! Judger, of course. But nobody is contributing a darn thing…if they would only…"

Joseph held up his hand. "Whoa! Hold on, my friend. When you're with your team, it sounds like you're listening with Judger ears and thinking with Judger questions like: Are they going to screw up again? and How are they going to disappoint me this time?"

"Sure, those sound like my questions. What else would I be asking…" I suddenly stopped. "Boy, I just stubbed my toe on the iron ring in the story you told me, didn't I?"

"You sure did. Good observation! And like the farmer, your first reaction was to go Judger—which is natural enough," Joseph said. "Now do what the farmer did next. Get curious. Ask yourself, 'What's happening here?' Think about your team, and this time follow the Learner path."

"Follow the Learner path with my team? You've got to be kidding," I said. "Besides, how would I do that?"

"For starters, listen to them with Learner ears. Reset yourself in Learner mindset before every meeting with your team. Try the kinds of questions Alexa asks, like: What do I appreciate about each of them? What are their best strengths? How can I help them collaborate most productively? How can we stay on the Learner path together?

"I'll bet you can see how those Learner questions would change everything in a meeting. Alexa's questions create a Learner environment. They invite everyone—including you—to listen more respectfully, with patience and care, and maybe even discover some gems in the process. With Learner questions we listen in order to understand the other person rather than to find out who's right or wrong. That makes it possible for everyone to get curious, feel safe taking risks, and participate fully, even when they're facing tough challenges."

"It's the tough challenges part that gets me in trouble," I argued. "We've got some big problems, and nobody is willing to speak up, much less take them on. Plus, there are so many major decisions we disagree on. We just can't seem to get through the conflicts to the other side. That's when I get frustrated and start feeling like nothing is ever going to work out. I think myself right down into the Judger Pit."

"Even though you'll never be pure Learner or a saint, including with your team, you can learn to choose where you put your attention moment to moment. Any attention you give to Judger isn't available to give to Learner. Accept Judger, practice Learner. Imprint those words on your brain. It's as important for teams as it is for individuals."

Accept Judger, practice Learner.
It's as important for teams as it is for individuals!

"So that's why Alexa's meetings are so great," I reflected. "They're Learner environments, as you say. I always have the sense that we have her full attention and that she really cares about what we have to say. If she ever goes Judger, I'm sure it's just for a fleeting visit." I had a sudden insight. "All she asks are Learner questions, and lots of them. Plus, I'll bet she gets an almost perfect score on asking questions and listening deeply and generously with just about everyone she knows. That's why she's called the Inquiring leader, isn't it?"

"That's it," Joseph said. "Alexa genuinely cares about what each person has to say and, of course, she's also genuinely curious. Not only does she ask Learner questions, but she also listens with Learner ears. Alexa's listening is focused by questions such as: What's valuable here? What's to be learned from that comment? How can this contribute to what we're working on? The questions she listens with help her teams turn into Learner teams very quickly. She expects to find the treasure, she looks for it, and because of that she often finds it.

"The Choice Map can help you do this with your team, too. Look at it again. So far, we've been thinking about it as a guide for how an individual thinks, behaves, and relates. Now, let's consider it as a guide for teams. Start thinking in terms of Learner teams and Judger teams.

"I think of Learner teams as being typically high performing, and Judger teams as being typically low performing. When researchers explored what distinguished high-performing teams from low-performing ones, can you guess what they found?"

Part of me didn't even want to know; another part was intrigued. But I decided not to guess. "No, what?" I replied.

"First of all, the high-performing teams had more positive emotions than the low-performing ones. That's not a big surprise. But what I found revealing was that the low-performing teams were low on inquiry—that is, on asking questions—and high on advocacy—that is, on pushing a particular viewpoint rather than listening to anybody else."

"So the bottom line," I said, "is if you want high performance, focus on Learner."

"Yes," Joseph said. "But there's more. The research also showed that high-performing teams consistently had a good balance between inquiry and advocacy—where people feel free to ask tough questions and have genuine open debate. They can even argue and have conflicts, yet the atmosphere remains essentially Learner."

"That's exactly what happens with Alexa's meetings," I said. "This is great!"

"It's what Alexa calls a Learner Alliance," Joseph said. "It's when team members work together to stay on the Learner path. That's the complete opposite of what happens when members of a team go Judger and end up polarized in what I call a Judger stand-off. That's when each person just defends their own opinion and believes they're the only one who is right. They turn deaf ears to anyone else's ideas. It's like everyone is in Judger jail together. Nothing gets done, and everyone blames someone else. That's the real cost of Judger when it takes over a team like that."

It's a Learner Alliance when team members work together to stay on the Learner path.

When I pictured the Choice Map, I could clearly imagine Alexa's whole team jogging happily along the Learner path, having set off on their journey with Learner questions. Their attention was free to focus on new solutions and possibilities. Alexa's team would certainly qualify as a high-performing one. And my team? Most of my people were down at the bottom of the map, mired in the mud of the Judger Pit—and I'd put them there! I hated to admit that most of the time I was being a Judger leader. But accepting that fact was the only way I'd ever get them out.

"I'm just the opposite of Alexa," I mumbled. "She seems to create a balanced Learner environment almost automatically."

"She models Learner Living for all of us," Joseph said. "But it's good to remember that she wasn't always that way. Like most of us, she was automatically more Judger to start with. It usually takes effort and intention to turn the tide and become more naturally Learner. Think about it as deliberately training your brain to do things it doesn't automatically know how to do. Like anything—learning to drive a car or operate a computer or learning to ride a bike—it requires close attention at first but soon becomes second nature."

"This is a lot to take in," I said. "When I first walked into your office, truthfully I was just looking for a quick fix. What you're offering is obviously a lot bigger."

Joseph nodded.

"Can't you narrow it down to a few words of advice?" I joked.

"How often do people really take advice?"

He was right, of course. "I guess I'm an expert at not taking advice."

"Aren't we all?" Joseph replied. "Even though it's hard to resist, I try to avoid giving advice. I know that if I ask good questions, people are smart enough to come up with their own best answers. Our own advice is the only kind most of us listen to and act on anyway.... But I do have a suggestion for you, Ben." Joseph flashed his signature mischievous grin. "Do you want to hear it?"

"Sure," I said—and we both laughed.

"Alexa is a great model for what you and I are working on. She went through a lot of things similar to what you've been through in order to accomplish what she has. Next time you meet with Alexa, ask her to tell you about her experiences. I'm sure she'd be happy to."

Good suggestion! I thought. Then I asked Joseph if there were any other things I should bring up with Alexa.

Joseph nodded. "There is something else. Alexa came up with this terrific Question Thinking practice she calls Q-Storming®. It's sort of like brainstorming except that you're looking for new questions instead of answers and ideas. Ask her to explain Q-Storming to you. There's also a tool about it in your Users Guide. Alexa credits Q-Storming with being the catalyst for many of her most important breakthroughs."

Now that sounded really intriguing—and promising. That's where Joseph and I ended our conversation that day.

Down on the street a few minutes later, I cut through the park across from the Pearl Building into an open playing field where an older boy was helping a younger one learn to ride his bicycle. I stopped to watch.

In spite of spills and near falls, they were having fun. There were shouts of encouragement, along with cries of despair as the younger boy made yet another mistake and tumbled to the ground. Each time the younger boy fell, the older one rushed to his side to give assistance and support to try again.

Finally, the younger boy caught on. He rode off, covering 50 feet or so, with the older boy chasing after him, whooping and hollering cries of victory. I caught myself thinking Why are adults so damned competitive? Why are they so uncooperative, always looking for ways to show up the other guy? Why did I have to put up with people like Charles? I was getting angry.

I turned around to catch one last glimpse of the kids before climbing into my car. Now the two of them were standing beside the upright bike, laughing together. The expressions on their faces told me everything. The new bike rider glowed with the excitement of having achieved something new. And this experience had triggered that universal I-did-that response that I must admit always gives me a glow. I reached for the ignition key and thought, wouldn't it be amazing if our team could work together just like those kids? I wonder what it would take to make that happen—to have everyone on our team experience the I-did-that response again and again.

At that moment I realized I'd done something that was still quite new for me. I had transformed Judger questions into Learner ones. Not bad, I thought. A chill of excitement ran up the whole length of my spine. I guess those kids weren't the only ones who could experience the pleasure of the I-did-that response. I couldn't wait to share this with Joseph. That's when it occurred to me that maybe I really could follow Alexa's example—turn my team into a Learner team by becoming a Learner leader. The Inquiring coach, as Alexa called Joseph, was really onto something! I wanted to find out what else Joseph had up his sleeve. I was beginning to feel real hope that maybe it wasn't too late to salvage my career.

CHAPTER 10

When the Magic Works

"When you enter a mindset, you enter a new world."

Carol S. Dweck

Over breakfast a few days later, Grace told me about what had happened with Jennifer, the young woman she'd been having so much trouble with at work. Grace even apologized for calling me during the day just to vent.

"I kept the Choice Map on my desk all day," Grace said. "Two Learner questions kept jumping out at me—What do I want for myself, for others, and for the situation? And What are my choices? When I applied those questions to Jennifer, I realized I wanted her to start showing more common sense and initiative. So, I tried some new questions. I asked myself Why does Jennifer need so much direction from me? I became truly curious after I realized I didn't know. Was she afraid of acting on her own? Or worried that I'd fire her for making a mistake? I also wondered whether she had more going for her than I'd given her credit for. The next time she came to me for help I asked her a question instead of just giving her instructions. I inquired with real curiosity, 'How would you solve this problem if you were the boss?'

"That single question opened up a very productive conversation. Jennifer confessed that she was, indeed, afraid of me. She thought if she didn't do exactly what I expected her to, I'd fire her. This is what had happened with her previous boss, and she didn't want it to ever happen again. That talk changed everything. She told me that afterward she felt more comfortable about taking initiative and working on her own. She also came up with some good ideas for solving her own problem. She was obviously very pleased with herself. I congratulated her—and told her how happy I was that we had opened up communication between us.

"I'm really surprised, and glad. And, you know what? Asking Learner questions made me feel a lot better at the end of the day. I realize now I was being unfair to Jennifer. I had been assuming she was asking all those questions because she was incompetent. She really isn't. It's just that she didn't feel safe with me. I think she believed she had to check everything out with me before acting on her own or taking risks. That crowded out any room for her to be creative or take any initiative."

As Grace told me the story of her breakthrough with Jennifer, I was relieved she didn't ask me about any results I'd gotten from working with Joseph's ideas. It's true I'd had some shifts in my thinking and was somewhat hopeful rather than just resigned. But I didn't have much to show for my efforts yet. And my team was still a nightmare.

When I finally left home I was at least 20 minutes late. Traffic was piling up on the freeway. A mile past my on-ramp, the highway had practically turned into a parking lot. Cars were creeping along for as far as I could see, and in all four lanes. I was getting frantic. I didn't even notice my Judger mindset had kicked in. At least not right away.

Then traffic stopped completely. I gritted my teeth, set the car in park, and pulled out my phone to check for messages. My secretary had texted several reminders, which did nothing to lessen my stress. I was already anxious about that morning's meeting with Alexa and was dreading the one with Charles this afternoon. I wasn't ready for either, least of all the latter.

I slapped the steering wheel in frustration, muttering something about how one guy, stupid enough to run out of gas, had ruined the whole day for half the city. Who was the idiot responsible? I didn't need this! Was it so difficult to keep your tank filled? Didn't that fool realize…

I felt like my head would explode if traffic didn't start moving. Tension spread through my whole body, like an electric sensation shooting out to every muscle. These sensations were all too familiar. Mostly I was aware of the muscles in my legs and back tensing up as if getting ready to fight or run, or maybe both, if that's possible. But here I was frozen to the spot, in traffic that gave no signs of moving…and I had to get to the office.

I suddenly stopped myself. Ben, you're solidly in Judger, I said, my voice muffled by the sounds of the idling engine. And then I actually laughed at myself. My observer self to the rescue! Could Judger really cause all those unpleasant physical symptoms? Could it be Judger feeding my frustration and these angry thoughts? This upset wasn't only in my head. That's for sure. It may have started as my own thoughts or feelings, but there wasn't a grain of doubt that

Judger affected every part of my body. I could almost feel it in my brain, clouding my thinking.

About then I heard sirens and a few minutes later an ambulance sped past in the emergency lane. Accident! I switched on the radio for the traffic report. Two people badly hurt. Oh, man! I was embarrassed about jumping to the conclusion that some jerk had run out of gas. Who was the real jerk—me! My attention then shifted to the people who were hurt. I hoped they were going to be okay. What was wrong with me, getting so worked up over a story I'd made up in my own mind? What a great reminder to not believe everything I think! I noticed that my stress softened a little as my thoughts focused on the victims of the crash: Will they get help soon enough? Are they in pain? How will this accident affect their lives?

Ten minutes later traffic still wasn't moving, and I must admit I started to get frustrated and stressed again. Worries about my meeting with Charles intruded. My thoughts churned around in my brain, fueling my longstanding annoyance with him. I sure needed help with this one! What would Joseph tell me? I heard his voice in my head, reminding me how important it is to change my questions, especially about Charles and my team.

Yesterday Joseph told me to find a real situation to test out what I'd been learning about recovering from a Judger hijack. The meeting with Charles this afternoon was about as real as it gets. But what questions would help me get out of what Grace called my Judger head? What Learner questions could help me with Charles? Traffic suddenly moved forward a hundred yards or so before it stopped again. In those few moments I realized I had already stepped onto the Switching Lane with the questions I'd just asked myself.

Joseph kept suggesting that whenever I was able to catch myself in Judger I should stop and congratulate myself for becoming more aware. Catching myself in Judger is a Learner move. Then I should step back and find out what I was asking myself. At that moment the question that popped into my mind was how can I get out of here? Obviously, there wasn't much choice about that. I was stuck until traffic started moving. Then something else Joseph said came back to me: "We don't have much control over what happens, but we can choose how we relate to what happens." Almost immediately, a new question came to mind: What can I do right now to make the best use of this time?

> We don't have much control over what happens, but we can choose how we relate to what happens.

It took only a second to come up with an answer to that one. I grabbed my phone off the seat beside me and scrolled to Joseph's number. He answered immediately.

"Ben here," I said. "Do you have a minute? I'm stuck in traffic and going a little nuts."

Joseph was silent for a moment, then laughed: "Did you try saying beam me up, Scotty?"

"How'd you know I was a Trekkie?" I laughed and almost instantly my mood lightened.

"I've got a meeting with Charles this afternoon," I explained. "I realize I have to get into Learner mindset to even have a chance of it going well. I'm worried that I'll blow it. Where do I begin?"

"Good question," Joseph said. "Can you write something down?"

"Sure," I said. "Go ahead."

As I sat there in stalled traffic, Joseph dictated three questions which I recorded on my smartphone: What assumptions am I making? How else can I think about this? And What is the other person thinking, feeling, and wanting? Joseph explained that these questions were from his Top 12 Questions for Success, one of the tools I'd find in the Users Guide.

I looked at the first question: What assumptions am I making? That was easy enough. Where Charles was concerned my assumptions were unavoidable. I'd beaten him out of a big promotion. Guys in that position can be dangerous. I'd be a fool to drop my guard with him. I was sure nothing would make Charles happier than to see me fail. I was also sure he'd do whatever he could to make that happen. Then he could step into my position and have what he wanted. Who wouldn't assume you had to watch your back with guys like that?

Ben's Three Questions

- What assumptions am I making?
- How else can I think about this?
- What is the other person thinking, feeling, and wanting?

Sure, these were just assumptions. I wasn't denying that. But there are situations where going with your assumptions is the safest route, and this was one of them. So far, the problems I was having with Charles seemed real enough to me. Only a fool would ignore them. As I thought about all this, something I'd read in the Learner/Judger Mindset Chart kept nagging at me: Was I defending my assumptions instead of questioning them?

Though still unsettled, I turned to Joseph's second question: How else can I think about this? Something Grace had said clicked in my mind—how her assumptions about Jennifer had damaged their relationship. Grace had used the Choice Map to find a different way of relating to Jennifer. Could I do the same with Charles?

I began to wonder about other possibilities. For example, what would happen if I reconsidered some of my opinions about Charles? What if his questions weren't aimed at making me look bad, as I'd assumed? What if he just wanted to make sure we'd covered all our bases? Then I remembered Joseph telling me about winning teams and their balance between inquiry and advocacy. What if Charles' endless questions were just his way to encourage more thoughtful discussions? I was pretty sure I was giving Charles more credit than he was due—but maybe I wasn't. The more I considered other ways of thinking about the situation, the less certain I was about my old opinions.

I decided to try something new in my meeting with Charles that afternoon. When he walked in, I would suspend thinking that he was after my job and out to sabotage me. Instead, I would try to be neutral, to adopt a mindset of not-knowing, as Joseph had suggested, rather than thinking I had to have all the answers. The moment this thought crossed my mind, new ideas tumbled into place. Even though I wasn't ready to totally trust Joseph's theories, for the first time I was willing to give Charles the benefit of the doubt. After all, questioning my assumptions wasn't ignoring them. It was exploring them. This was great. Now I had something that was new, that was innovative, and that I could do.

I was just starting to consider Joseph's third question—What is the other person thinking, feeling, and wanting?—when traffic began to inch forward. I put that question on hold. But even as I got under way, new possibilities began unfolding in my mind. If Charles was merely being inquisitive, what was he wanting or needing from me? I remembered a conversation we'd had my first day on the job. He'd said, "I have to tell you, I'm disappointed I didn't get the promotion. This is a great company, and my family likes this town. I don't want to have to move them. I'll do everything I can to make this company successful."

His comment that he could do anything to make this company successful still bothered me. What exactly did he mean by that? My assumption had been that this included going after my job. Could I have misread Charles' intentions? Could there be another way of interpreting what he'd said?

I arrived at my office way behind schedule. With less than 10 minutes before my meeting with Alexa, I sat down at my computer, typed in her name and that of the magazine I'd seen in Joseph's Hall of Fame gallery. The article about her popped up instantly. I scanned the story. It told about her stepping into the CEO position at KB right after it went into Chapter 11. She had been brought in to turn the company around. Everyone had advised her against it. If she didn't succeed, it could destroy her career. She took the risk and accomplished the impossible, and three years later she took the company global.

I skipped ahead several paragraphs. Alexa was quoted as saying she owed her success to "simply changing the kinds of questions I was asking." In the next paragraph she named her personal coach and mentor: Joseph S. Edwards. Who else?

Moments after reading the article, I was seated in Alexa's office. Although my intention was to ask about her experiences with Joseph and about Q-Storming, my curiosity got the best of me and I found myself asking about the article. "You never told me about your getting the Woman of the Year award," I said. "I just read about it on the Internet."

"Oh, yes. They labeled me The Inquiring Leader. You know what? I don't think my interviewer had ever heard of a CEO making a point of asking lots of questions. It was a great novelty to him!" She chuckled at the thought. "It seems like such a simple thing. Most leaders do more telling than asking. That's why they never find out what's really going on. All too often they base their decisions about strategic direction, and even about their own people, on insufficient or inaccurate information."

"They make assumptions instead," I added, "which they never test."

"Exactly. Well, that just didn't make any sense to me."

I heard Joseph's teachings in her words, but what she said was obviously authentic for her.

"Joseph and I have been discussing Learner and Judger mindsets and the Choice Map," I said. "He told me I'm not the only person in this room who ever ran into problems with Judger."

I checked her expression to make sure she didn't mind my saying that. She was smiling, so I continued. "He suggested you might share a few of your own Judger challenges with your old company. What were some of the Judger questions you started out with?"

"You know, in retrospect it seems so simple I almost laugh. The kinds of questions I'd been asking were along the order of who's to blame for the mess we're in? I was lying awake nights trying to figure out whom I should fire—and worrying that it might be me! Then, one day, working with Joseph, I started coming up with new questions. I think the first one was how can we avoid making so many mistakes? Joseph thought that was a good beginning but suggested I could come up with something even better."

"You mean a stronger Learner question?"

"Exactly," Alexa said. "The one I figured out was How can we build on our strengths and successes? I really took that question seriously and started asking it all the time. I got everyone on track with that new question. I could see that the Judger questions I'd been asking made everything more difficult. We had had what I'd call a high Judger culture. Judger drained our energy, pretty much killed our enthusiasm, divided us so we were always looking for someone to blame—in short, Judger derailed us and had us going in all directions at once, none of which were very productive. That new Learner question piqued our curiosity and invited us to take positive, focused, and creative actions together. Joseph said to use the new question to build a Learner culture, and that's what I set out to do. Pretty soon we were turning things around in remarkable ways. Until then, I'd never really grasped the truth about the power of questions, that they can lead us to failure or to success. It was a big shift for me, and for all of us."

"What was it about that new question that made such a difference?" I asked.

"Maybe an example Joseph gave us would make this clearer. It had to do with a study that was done with two comparable basketball teams. Team A was coached with an emphasis on preventing mistakes on the court. Day after day, they reviewed videos that focused on their errors. Those mistakes got grooved in their brains. By contrast, Team B was coached with an emphasis on building on their successes. Day after day, they reviewed videos that focused on their most successful plays. So, the point is that Team B's successes got grooved into their brains.

"To put it simply, Team A focused on what was wrong. Team B focused on what was right. I'm sure you can guess which team had the greatest improvement by the end of the season."

"The one that built on their successes, of course."

"That's absolutely right," Alexa said. "In fact, by the end the difference in these teams' performances was startling. As I recall, Team A actually had a slight reduction in their accomplishments. Team B improved by nearly 30 percent. That's all it took to convince me of the power of asking the right kinds of questions, by which I mean Learner questions. I applied those same principles to our floundering company, and that's when dramatic changes began to occur. Not only did our productivity increase, but coming to work was more enjoyable, even fun. Creativity and morale were boosted. There was higher energy throughout the company. The whole place began operating on Learner principles and shifting to

Learner questions—the way that Learner begets Learner—and it all happened in months instead of years. I guess you just read the rest of the story."

Alexa paused as she recalled that time of her life. "What could be more natural or obvious," she continued, "than to simply ask? How else can you get a complete picture of what's going on? How else can you get people contributing so enthusiastically? What else would make people feel respected— and that what they said and did really mattered? Could we ever discover or learn or create anything new without being curious first? Curiosity is one of our greatest assets. I'm sure Joseph has emphasized this to you. Curiosity is the fast track to Learner. It's high-test fuel for progress and change!"

Curiosity is the fast track to Learner.

As Alexa talked, I was thinking about how important it was to check my assumptions about Charles. Were my Judger questions blinding me from seeing something important about him? Did I really know why Charles asked so many questions? Before I had a chance to stop myself the words popped out of my mouth.

"He's just asking me all those questions because he's curious. He wants to understand!"

Alexa looked at me with concern. "What in heaven's name are you talking about?"

"Sorry, Alexa, I was just thinking out loud," I replied. "This conversation has really gotten me all fired up about my team and our project."

"It sure seems that you're onto something," Alexa said, nodding her head. "And I think I can say with confidence that your new questions are going to produce some real progress."

My mind ran back to the conversation Grace and I had had earlier that morning. In working out her situation with Jennifer, Grace had started by asking herself: What do I want? and What are my choices? and then she asked: How can I understand her better? I realized this last question wasn't one I ever asked myself about people I worked with. Instantly, other questions popped into my mind: How does anyone ever understand anyone else? Joseph claimed you have to start by getting curious about them. And then you ask them questions, Learner questions, of course. This is exactly what Grace had done with Jennifer. What did I really understand about Charles? I began to feel my curiosity growing and realized new questions about him were naturally coming to mind.

I remembered that old question I'd reported to Joseph so proudly: How can I prove I'm right? Now I realized how that question had contributed to the team's perception of me as a know-it-all. Instead of asking how can I prove I'm right, I asked how can I better understand Charles, and how can I better understand my team? I was already beginning to see Charles and the team in a whole new light. What a contrast there was not only between those two questions but also in my mood and in how I was thinking about Charles!

Suddenly I remembered about Q-Storming. "Before I forget,"

I said. "Joseph suggested I ask you about Q-Storming. He said it was responsible for some of the best breakthroughs in your career."

Alexa's eyebrows went up. She sat forward and smiled. "It's one of my favorite subjects," she said. "You've heard of brainstorming, I'm sure. Q-Storming is like that, except you're looking for new questions, not for answers. It's a great way to get everyone on the same page, thinking collaboratively and out of the box. I've used it to get new thinking for all kinds of reasons: for decision making, problem solving, innovation, and even conflict resolution. I've mostly used it with groups and teams, but I've also discovered how helpful it can be in one-on-one conversations."

At that moment, the phone rang on Alexa's desk. "I may have to take this," she said. "I told my secretary not to interrupt us unless a certain call came in." She reached across the desk, picked up the phone, pressed it to her ear, and exchanged a few words with her assistant. Then she shrugged apologetically and covered the receiver as she told me it was indeed the call she'd been waiting for.

On the way back to my office, I was disappointed that I hadn't learned more about Q-Storming, but I was still eager to do so. Alexa seemed like living proof that there really was some magic in Joseph's theories. Was a little of it starting to rub off on me, too? That day still held some surprises, and the person who would coach me through Q-Storming was to be the biggest surprise of all.

CHAPTER 11

Q-Storming to the Rescue

"Ultimately, true questions are carried like lanterns that we swing in the dark to help us find our way."

Mark Nepo

With less than half an hour to get ready for my appointment with Charles, I went into self-coaching mode and focused on the three questions Joseph had given me that morning: What assumptions am I making? How else might I think about this? And, what is the other person thinking, feeling, and wanting?"

Then my secretary buzzed, announcing Charles' arrival. In the past, I would have kept him waiting. Today, I immediately got up and met him at the door. We shook hands, and I asked him how he was doing. He replied that he was fine, but he looked a little nervous. At least I wasn't the only one! When I originally made the appointment with him, I'd been all set for a showdown. Since then, my perspective on the problems between us had changed considerably. I offered him a comfortable chair and asked if he'd like coffee or anything to drink. That must have surprised him because I'd never done that in the past. He thanked me but said he was fine, holding up a small bottle of water he'd brought along.

Yesterday while thinking about this meeting, I reviewed many of the things I'd learned from Joseph. I also considered details about how Joseph and Alexa conducted their meetings with me. They had asked lots of questions and had a way of speaking that put me at ease. I always felt like they were on my side, that they wanted me to succeed. When I thought about it, I realized that both of them had made our meetings Learner experiences.

I'd recalled, for example, that Joseph made sure there wasn't a desk or other physical barrier between us. This gesture made me feel that he was truly interested in what I had to say. So I decided to do the same thing with Charles. With so much at stake, I wanted to do everything I could to make our meeting successful. I slid my chair from behind my desk and placed it so Charles and I were comfortably facing each other just a few feet apart near the window. Without the desk between us, establishing my authority, I felt a bit vulnerable. At first, Charles seemed a bit uncomfortable, too.

"I'm very worried about how our team is doing," I began. "In fact, we're really in trouble, so I'd like to talk some things through with you. And if it's okay, can we start with a few questions?"

Charles nodded.

"Let me be quite candid with you," I continued, trying to think how Joseph would say this. "I've realized that I may have contributed to some of the problems we've been having with our team. I want to change that, and I believe the place to start is with you and me."

I paused, checking out Charles' reaction. As far as I could tell, he was attentive and engaged, though he didn't look very relaxed. When I put myself in his place, it was easy to imagine what might be going through his mind. I continued, "I've made certain judgments about you that I now believe were wrong interpretations. For example, I knew you'd been at QTec for several years and that you were in line for the job that was given to me. I'm pretty sure my arrival wasn't exactly good news for you, and I assumed you'd have trouble working under me. Am I right about this?"

Charles nodded. "I've got to confess that it has been difficult. Alexa broke it to me gently enough, and made a nice salary adjustment, but that only goes so far."

His response surprised me. Had he already recognized the problem…and had he actually been working on it? It appeared so. For a moment I got defensive and guarded, thinking that if this were so maybe he should have gotten the job instead of me.

"Had the situation been reversed, I'd have been pretty bent out of shape myself," I said.

"I'm still working it out," Charles admitted. Let me ask you this." He paused. "How am I doing?"

"Considering that I put an awful lot off on you that really didn't belong on your shoulders, I think you're doing great."

"I'm not sure I understand," Charles said.

It wasn't easy saying what I said then. "I made a few assumptions about you, Charles. First, I assumed that because I was brought in over you that you'd resent me and wouldn't be able to work with me. I realize I was judging you unfairly. My second assumption had to do with all those questions you ask in our meetings."

"My questions?" Charles looked totally confused. A second or two later he had gathered his thoughts enough to say, "I don't get it. Why would my questions be a problem? You're the new guy. I need to find out what you want, where you're going to take us. How would I find out what I don't know if I don't ask?"

> ## How would I find out what I don't know if I don't ask?

I wasn't ready to admit to him that I'd thought his questions were aimed at showing others on the team that I didn't have all the answers. However, I told him that my job at QTec required a huge shift in the way I was accustomed to operating. "At my old company," I explained, "people came to me for answers. I was so good at it that I earned a sterling reputation as the answer man. Here at QTec I'm heading up a team and I need other people to help me find answers and implement them. Being the answer man isn't enough."

Charles took a sip of water from his bottle, then said, "A few weeks before you came aboard, Alexa brought in this guy for a training session. It was about just this sort of thing, about questions and answers. He talked about the profound power of questions, how they can help us to become more innovative and change our thinking, our relationships, our teams, and even an entire organization. He asked us how anyone could expect to get the best answers without first asking the best questions. One thing he said stands out in my memory. It was: Great results begin with great questions."

I remembered Alexa telling me about that training session the day she hired me. She explained how she was having Joseph come in to facilitate a core training on Question Thinking. She'd invited me to attend, but I'd had scheduling conflicts with my old employer and couldn't make it. Besides, I was the answer man! Questions were the last thing on my mind back then. On top of that I barely knew what I was going to do as the leader of my team. I couldn't help but wonder how things might have turned out had I attended Joseph's training that day. There was no doubt in my mind that Charles was describing that training, so it seemed safe to assume he also had some familiarity with Question Thinking and the Learner and Judger mindset material.

"Since I wasn't there," I said, a bit apprehensively, "maybe you'd suggest ways that you see us employing some of Joseph's practices here." The moment those words left my mouth I regretted it. Was I going too far and undercutting my own authority? Was this giving Charles what he wanted? Meanwhile, he had folded his hands in his lap. His head was slightly bowed as if he was thinking about ways to answer that question. Finally, he looked up, drew a deep breath and said, "Every question missed is a potential crisis waiting to happen."

> Every question missed is a potential crisis waiting to happen.

"I'm not sure I understand," I said. "Could you say more?"

"It's one of the things Joseph told us, to emphasize the importance of Question Thinking, and asking questions in general,"

Charles said. "He even handed out cards with that sentence printed on it. I've pinned one of those cards to my bulletin board as a reminder."

"I guess maybe our team has been missing a lot of questions about our project," I said. The room went silent. I wasn't sure what to do or say next. All I could think of was that I hadn't until now invited questions from my team. On the contrary, I'd squelched them. I'd been interpreting Charles' questions as criticisms of me. I'd reacted defensively and made a Judger mess of my team. If Joseph's saying was really true, my reactions had led to a lot of unasked questions. Was I to blame for my team's lack of participation? What was wrong with me? Why had it taken me so long to see this? Judger questions tumbled around in my mind. It didn't take a genius to see who was at fault. But I couldn't stop here. If I wanted to move forward and find real solutions, I had to accept what was true and start asking very different kinds of questions— Learner questions, and lots of them. What's more, I had to start encouraging questions from all my team members.

"I need your help," I said. Instantly, I was surprised by the tone of confidence that came through in my voice. "As you know, it's the eleventh hour for our project. If we don't get off the dime and move forward, we're in real trouble."

Charles nodded. "I understand," he said. "And I share your concerns. You have my full pledge that I'm behind you 110 percent."

"That means a lot to me," I said, convinced he was sincere in his pledge. "Let's start with this question: How do we get past what's been blocking us and our team?" This was a question I'd come up with in my preparations for this meeting. "In particular, what do you need to help us be successful?"

For a moment, Charles seemed taken aback. Then he said, "I'm not sure I have any immediate answers or even the best questions. However, I am sure of one thing—that whatever we're doing in this conversation feels a whole lot better than before. It seems like a good direction." He paused, then added, "I think I've got something that could be helpful to us."

My hackles went up. Here he goes again, I thought, reacting like I had a million times before. He's going to challenge my authority. But I quickly stopped myself. In that instant three Self-Q's popped into my mind: Am I in Judger? How else can I think about this? What do I want to accomplish in this meeting? If I wanted to clear the air with Charles and get the team moving forward, I had to let go of my old assumptions. Everything depended on it.

"I'm all ears," I said.

"It's something Joseph showed us," Charles said. "He called it Q-Storming."

At that moment you could have knocked me over with a feather. Just a day before I would have done anything to shut Charles down. Today I just said, "Tell me about it."

Charles got up and went over to the flipchart that had become a permanent fixture in my office and picked up a blue felt-tip marker. "The goal," he explained, "is not to come up with answers, ideas, or solutions. Instead we want to come up with as many new questions as possible. Just throw out questions as fast as we can, while I write them down."

"In other words, with no responses or discussion in between," I guessed.

"Exactly. Joseph said the goal is to open new doors in our minds…behind every door we might find another answer or solution. Every new question just expands our range of possibilities. I think his exact words were 'A question not asked is a door not opened.'

A question not asked is a door not opened.

"You always start by describing the problematic situation and your goals for change," Charles explained. "After that you figure out what assumptions you have about the situation."

"You mean like the assumption I made that you'd have trouble working with me," I said.

Charles cringed but then nodded. "Once you've got your goals and assumptions clarified, you look at the facts about the situation. After that you start brainstorming new questions. For example, you might ask: In what ways can we best work together to meet our targets?" He wrote that question on the flipchart. After that, he immediately added another question: What do I want to change about the team?

"What don't we want to change!" I exclaimed.

"Joseph says the secret of successful Q-Storming is to stay in Learner and be careful about how you phrase the questions," Charles continued. "If we're to get the results we want, the questions need to be in the first person…in other words, asking in terms of I or we. That helps us open doors in our own minds."

"Okay," I said. "You mean like: What would I like to happen that isn't happening now? How can we all listen better? What can I do to be more creative?"

"Great questions," Charles said, writing as fast as he could and underlining all the I's and we's.

I'm not sure where it came from, but right after he said this, a new question popped out of my mouth: How can I keep the communication channels open between you and me and our other team members?

I thought I saw Charles smile, but he didn't say anything, just wrote my last question on the flipchart. Then he added another of his own: What will help me to keep asking the right kinds of questions?

How do we state our goals better, so everybody can be more aligned?

"And inspired?" Charles added.

"Exactly," I said.

"Let's keep going. More questions!" Charles exclaimed. He continued to jot them down on the flipchart, scrawling them out with the blue felt-tip pen:

—*What kind of fuel can I bring to keep our team running?*

—*How can we remind ourselves about failure as feedback?*

—*How do I keep from being judgmental?*

—*What are the greatest strengths of each team member?"*

—*How do we make sure we follow through on all our promises?*

—*How can I assure each and every member it's okay to take risks?*

—*How do I assure them it's also fine to ask for help?*

We both fired off questions in rapid succession. I was surprised at how naturally and easily Charles and I were working together. In no time we had four sheets covered with questions, and they were all over the floor. Finally, I suggested we stop and review what we'd done.

Charles stepped back from the flipchart and said, "Joseph explained that it was important to notice if there are any questions we hadn't asked before. The new questions can make the biggest difference."

I quickly looked over the list still on the flipchart and shuffled through the sheets of questions on the floor. "Yes, quite a few," I admitted, frankly startled at how many I really hadn't asked.

Charles and I stood in front of the flipchart and then taped the other sheets up on the wall. We spent the next half hour looking over all our questions and adding new ones here and there. As we began discussing the questions it became clearer to me why we'd been stuck and what would help us make the changes we needed.

Seeing all those questions written down also helped me slip into self-coaching mode and look at my present situation more objectively. Q-Storming allowed me to see possibilities I never would have come up with on my own. I remembered Alexa's story about her big breakthrough, how changing the kinds of questions she asked had changed the whole company. I was getting an inkling of how that could happen for us as well.

Charles was copying our questions with his phone for later reference.

I perched on the edge of my desk, staring at the flipchart. "I think I have a question to add to our list," I said. I went up to the chart, turned to a new sheet and wrote: *—What will help each of us make our best contribution?*

"Nice," Charles said, nodding.

That word *contribution* suddenly became the focus of my attention. In my zeal to assert my old role as the answer man, I had hardly ever asked questions such as: *What do other people have to offer? What do they need and want? What is my effect on them?* I saw even more deeply how the failure of the team, the team I used to call a nightmare, had been the leader of the team: me! I had been the problem all along!

"I think I could spend the next few hours discussing what we've just accomplished here," I said. "But do you know what the most valuable lessons are for me in all of this?"

Charles shook his head.

"First, this was a great demonstration that questions have the power to open things up and maybe even turn things around. I can imagine using Q-Storming with the team—and as soon as possible! Second, I've got a whole new perspective on the ways that questions can help us better appreciate and understand the people around us."

These revelations were opening another very big door for me, with a new question coming into sharp focus: *Am I willing to allow others to help me or contribute to solving our problems?*

"Ben," Charles said. "Before this meeting, I wasn't at all sure I would be able to stay on here at QTec. To tell the truth, working with you had started feeling like it was more trouble than it was worth."

"That painful, huh?" I did my best to cover up how ill at ease his statement made me feel. I even felt the tug of defensiveness. But then something shifted inside me. I felt my face break into an embarrassed grin, then I just laughed out loud. "I sympathize with you entirely," I said.

"Sorry, I guess I came off pretty harsh, didn't I?" Charles said. "But I needed to tell you that."

"Yes, you did," I said. "We both needed that." I extended my hand to him. He hesitated for just a second and then shook it warmly. We had made our peace, and it felt great. In the process I'd made the breakthrough I'd been hoping for—and changing my questions was the pivot that made the difference. I could hardly wait to tell Joseph what had happened.

After Charles left my office, I went back to the flipchart and started blocking out plans for meeting with our team the following morning. This time I wanted to have the right questions so that Learner Living could take root for our team. That would change everything about the way we worked together. I was sure our results would change because of that. I sat down at my desk, pulled out my notes from my meetings with Joseph and began thumbing through them.

I leaned back in my chair and stared at the little placard on the wall: "Question everything!" Yes, I thought, Joseph was right. It all seemed so simple now. Right. Simple—like Einstein's Theory of Relativity!

CHAPTER 12

Amour! Amour!

"Out beyond ideas of wrongdoing and rightdoing, there is a field.
I'll meet you there."

Rumi

That night, charged up by all that had happened in the meetings with Alexa and Charles, I worked late. In fact, I worked till long after dark, making notes for the meeting the next morning with Charles and the team. I also sent an email to Alexa to check on Joseph's availability for meeting with us within the next few weeks. Time raced by. When I remembered to check the clock, it was two hours past the time I told Grace I'd be home. I considered calling but figured she'd be in bed sound asleep, so I decided not to disturb her. On the way home in the car I noticed it was going on eleven o'clock.

When I walked in the house, I found Grace sitting alone in the dimly lit living room. She was in her pajamas, reading by a single lamp beside her chair. The moment I greeted her, I knew something was wrong. She silently set aside her book, walked up to me, took my hand, led me over to the sofa, and gently told me to sit down. I sat, half expecting her to announce that someone had died—or that she was leaving me. She perched herself on the arm of the overstuffed chair across from me, leaned slightly forward and gazed into my eyes. This was going to be serious.

"Ben," she said, "you have got to tell me what's going on with you."

Just as I'd done so many times before, my first instinct was to shrug it off. "I worked late. I told your secretary…. I considered calling but figured you were asleep."

"It's not about that. You know it isn't." She fixed me with a look that told me she wasn't going to back off.

"There's been a lot of pressure at work…deadlines coming up way too fast…but I think there was some real progress today… nothing to worry about." I knew I was waffling, but to tell the truth I was scared half to death.

Grace shook her head slowly, paused, then asked, "What is it you need right now?"

For a moment I was speechless. Wasn't this the very question I'd asked myself about Charles? What does the other person need and want? Was she reading my mind, or had she somehow seen Joseph's Top 12 Questions for Success?

"What do I need?" I echoed nervously. "You know, at this point I'm not even sure." I wasn't lying to her. I really didn't know.

"Okay, let me tell you what I've been noticing," Grace began. "Not long after you took this job, our whole relationship changed. You changed. I began to worry it was something about me. Did you suddenly feel that marrying me had been a mistake? Had I done something that offended or hurt you?"

I held up my hand. "Oh, Grace, it isn't anything like that, not at all!" The idea that I had been so oblivious to her feelings made me want to weep.

"That's what I realized after studying the Choice Map," she said. "You know what became clear—we've both been going down the Judger path. I know I've been judging myself and you, and I see you being in Judger, too."

I had been bursting to tell her about my breakthrough with Charles, how it had already changed so much for me at work. Suddenly even that faded into the background. I searched for words to tell Grace how sorry I was to have caused her such pain. But all I could do at first was nod and say I agreed with her.

"I'm filled with questions about us," Grace continued. "But until this afternoon my questions were mostly Judger ones. Then I started looking for things I might do or say to keep us from getting stuck in the Judger Pit."

"This is really hard for me to hear," I said, bowing my head, "I guess there's no easy way to say this…no other way through it…" I prayed I wasn't going to lose it.

Grace suddenly looked as pale as a ghost. "Please let this not be what I'm thinking," she said, her voice shaky and fearful.

"What?" An alarm went off in my head. All sorts of possibilities raced through my mind. She leaned forward from the arm of her chair, staring at me. I took a deep breath. "Wait," I blurted out. "What are you thinking? You don't think…"

"It's all the long nights you've spent at the office, all the excuses for not coming home, failing to call even to let me know where you were, not having time for me…for us." She paused. "What did you expect me to think?"

"Grace…I swear, it's nothing like that." This was really tough! It had never occurred to me that she might have interpreted my long hours at work like this.

I shook my head slowly, partly because I couldn't believe what I was hearing and partly to assure her I was not having an affair. "I would never do that, Grace." I paused and gave a lot of thought to what I was going to say next. "There's something I want to tell you that I'm finding very difficult to say. I hope you won't end up hating me for it...maybe even as much as if there'd been another woman."

My face felt hot and my voice sounded shaky. I had no idea what Grace's reaction would be in the next few moments. I was afraid that she might even walk out on me when I told her the truth about my failures at work.

"I didn't exactly tell you the truth about Joseph and how I got the Choice Map," I began. "I was in a real jam at work. Things were not going well at all. As I saw it, I had to choose between going to Joseph for executive coaching or handing in my resignation."

"Your resignation! Is that what this is all about? Oh, Ben, I'm so sorry!"

"For months I've been afraid I wasn't cut out to be a leader. Just the opposite! Everything I tried just seemed to get crappy results. I was letting down everyone who'd believed in me, you as well as Alexa. And certainly the team I was supposed to be leading! And if this job didn't work out...well, I was afraid of how it would affect us...you and me. Frankly, I was afraid you'd think I wasn't good enough for you."

We were both silent for several moments, then she asked quietly, "When did you first realize things weren't working out in the new job?"

"A few weeks into it," I confessed. "At first it was great. I really thought I could handle the leadership thing. Then I was hit with one challenge after another that I couldn't manage, until I felt like I was drowning…I just couldn't find the answers."

"Wait," she interrupted. "You've had all of that going on for all this time and you never told me about it?"

"You're angry, Grace, aren't you? I just knew it was going to turn out like this. I'm really sorry. But I think things are turning around for me, in fact, I'm sure of it…"

"Wait a second," Grace said. "Back up. You knew what? What did you think was going to turn out like this? Do you know why I'm angry at you? Are you sure you know why?"

"Of course I do. For screwing up at this job."

"No! No! No! That's not it at all!" She practically shouted this at me.

"Then for what?" I asked, totally taken aback. Had she found some offense that was even worse, something I didn't even know about yet? I wracked my brain for an explanation.

"What I'm upset about is that you've kept your problems a secret from me. You're my husband, and you didn't let me know about something this important to both of us."

"I had every intention of telling you but only after I got things rolling again. I was pretty sure I could get a new job right away, things would get better, and you would never have to know."

"In other words, you were going to continue trying to cover this up and keep me in the dark." Suddenly she looked like she wanted to punch me. "Good grief, Ben, how could you be so clueless?"

I stared back at her like she was a stranger. I really didn't know what to say.

"Listen to me," she said. "You better get what I'm about to say, or we're never going to make it. I want you to share what's real with me, your troubles, your doubts, your victories, all of it. I need you to. That's such an important part of marriage for me. That's what helps me feel connected. When I'm having trouble at work, I talk it over with you, don't I?"

"Sure. I guess you do. I never thought about it."

"You never thought about it! Are you kidding me? Do you remember what I asked you when you came in tonight?"

"Yes, you asked me what I needed."

"You haven't answered me," she said. "I need you to do that. I want you to. Right now."

My jaw dropped and I just stared into Grace's eyes for a long time. I don't know how much time passed. Maybe it was just seconds, but those moments are imprinted in my mind forever. What do you need? Those four words, asked with so much loving care, were like laser beams cutting through a stone wall I hadn't even known I had erected around me, around my heart.

"What I want…" I began, "I guess if I'm being totally honest right now, I want to tell you everything that's been happening to me and not let my fears stop me."

I paused to check out Grace's expression before continuing. She was smiling but there was something else in her face that I couldn't quite read. In spite of that, I had to press on.

"I've had to confront my own limitations," I began, working up my courage. "I've spent way too much time in Judger and have made a lot of assumptions—hurtful ones—about myself as well as other people. All of this has caused major problems at work.

And one of the toughest parts I've had to face is that…well, there's more to life than being the answer man. I've got a huge amount to learn. At least now I've got some better choices, thanks to our friend Joseph."

At that point, I poured out the whole story of what I'd gone through in the past few months, how I'd been scared to death that if I didn't succeed in this new position, Alexa would conclude that I couldn't make it as a leader at QTec. There had been so many days I'd felt like a failure that I didn't dare admit I was sliding faster and deeper into the Judger Pit. When I got to the end of my story, Grace got up from the arm of the chair where she'd been sitting. She came over and sat down in my lap, enfolding my head in her arms.

"I love you very much," she said. "I love you even more because of all that you've just shared with me. But promise me that you'll never hold out on me again. Promise?"

"It's not going to be easy," I told her. "Habits are hard to break. Besides, at work I've learned that you don't get ahead by whining."

"You're not whining! There's a huge difference between being a crybaby and being honest. We should always be open to asking each other what's going on and feel safe about telling the truth. Remember we're in this together."

There it was again—Learner Living—creating room for people to ask questions openly and to listen generously. This conversation was taking the breakthrough I'd had at work to a whole new level. Did I fully understand it all yet? I didn't. But what I did see, quite clearly, was that Joseph's methods worked as well at home as they did at work.

I don't remember the exact words I used though I do remember telling Grace how much this conversation meant to me. I thanked her for asking the questions she had, for listening to my problems, and for putting up with me during a very difficult time.

Grace kissed me gently on the lips. In that instant, I knew something important had changed, not just between Grace and me but in the whole way I looked at the world.

As we headed for the stairs that night, our arms were still around each other, making it difficult to walk. We laughed as we stumbled comically on the first steps. I told her I didn't want to let go but we'd never make it to the top entwined like this.

She smiled playfully, "But we could try!"

We kissed again and I suddenly got serious: "Can I ask you a question?"

"Anytime," Grace said, with a sparkle in her eyes. "Just anytime at all."

CHAPTER 13

Coming Full Circle

"Learning is the strength of strengths,
since it's the one that grows the rest of them."

Rick Hanson

Sitting at my desk this afternoon, I leaned back in my chair and reflected on all we had accomplished at QTec. In my right hand I held the rosewood paperweight Joseph had given me several years ago. Once again, I read the words on its sterling silver plaque: Great results begin with great questions. Those words and everything I'd learned from Joseph had become my inner compass, my personal GPS. Question Thinking had opened a part of my mind I might never have otherwise discovered, guiding me safely through some pretty rough terrain.

My mind drifted back to that dark day when I drafted my resignation letter, certain I hadn't lived up to Alexa's expectations and believing that she wanted to let me go. I had prepared a careful statement, thanking her for the trust she'd placed in me and acknowledging I wasn't the right person for the job. I just didn't have the leadership skills she was looking for, and I didn't know where to even start developing them. While mentally rehearsing how I would handle the actual meeting with her, Judger questions had filled my mind: What was wrong with me? What had made me think I could succeed as a leader? How could I tell Grace I had screwed up so badly?

As you already know, what happened in that meeting with Alexa was quite different from what I'd feared. To my surprise she'd refused to even read my resignation letter. Instead, she had referred me to Joseph for executive coaching. When she described what he did I was skeptical, but Alexa was so enthusiastic I couldn't refuse. She handed me his business card and I instantly spotted that big question mark on it. How could I miss it? It nearly leapt off the card! I'd hoped Alexa hadn't noticed how I'd rolled my eyes. I was convinced this guy couldn't help me. I'd built my reputation on being the answer man, and Alexa was recommending somebody specializing in a method called "Question Thinking." What could she be thinking? No way could this work for me.

I was in for a big surprise. When I put Joseph's system to the test, it produced excellent results for me. And while it wasn't easy to accept this fact, it soon became clear that that Judger mindset of mine had been jamming up the works for a very long time. The more Judger I was with my team, the more they seemed to resist everything I tried. I think it was soon after this realization that I began communicating with them—on purpose—from what Joseph calls Learner mindset. At the same time, I started asking more and telling less. Rather quickly it became apparent that things were turning around for us and we were starting to see the collaborative spirit that characterizes our team today.

By cultivating my Learner mindset, the contentious, adversarial relationship I'd had with Charles changed dramatically. Thanks to the Choice Map and Q-Storming, we rather easily navigated beyond the rough waters that had developed between us. And as Charles' and my working relationship got smoother and smoother, the methods we were employing caught on with those around us. Early on I'd believed everyone on my team would have to change before things improved. It turned out that the only person I had to change was me! Charles and my relationship became one of the most productive and innovative collaborations I have ever experienced. One thing was certain, my leadership of our team, and getting our product to market before the competition, couldn't have happened without Joseph's coaching—and without those changes in me.

Some months after the successful launch of our product, Joseph and I met for lunch, and he reminded me of that day I got stuck in traffic and called him up in frustration.

"It's nice to know that my agitation and frustration in the car that day—to say nothing of my whole body tightening up—wasn't just my imagination," I said in response. "It was all my amygdala's fault!"

Joseph laughed.

"Still," I continued, "you can't deny that the whole thing was compounded by being late for that meeting with Charles, which I was really dreading."

"What was it that changed what you were experiencing that day?" Joseph asked.

"It was those three Switching questions you gave me: *What assumptions am I making? How else can I think about this? What is the other person thinking, feeling, and wanting?* As soon as I began asking them, something shifted inside me. Those Switching questions helped me to get into my Learner mindset. I felt like I'd been released from the grip of all those Judger feelings."

"Where did your focus go at that point?"

"It shifted to Charles, but I was asking very different questions than I had before. I wasn't in Judger about him. Instead, I was consciously asking Learner questions about my own assumptions. And I was feeling much calmer, no longer stuck in that rut about Charles being my nemesis."

"Had anything changed outside you? Had the traffic changed? Had the problems you've been facing changed? Had Charles changed?"

"No, nothing outside me had changed. Traffic still wasn't moving. But those questions of yours changed how I was relating to the whole situation. By the time I got to my meeting I was feeling fairly confident that I could have a more productive conversation with Charles. And as you already know, that is exactly what happened. That meeting with him turned out to be a real breakthrough."

Joseph was looking as pleased as I felt.

"When I was beginning to develop this work," he said, "I was particularly interested in how far off the mark our responses can get when we let those primal reactions of the amygdala pull our strings. I guess you could say it's my passion to create tools and methods that enhance our capacity of choice with our reactions to the amygdala—though I didn't think of it in those terms at the time. I was thinking mostly in terms of self-management.

"What today I call Question Thinking goes hand in hand

with good leadership, fostering environments that are constructive, collaborative, and creative. Through the years one of my greatest rewards has been to witness how QT tools and strategies help leaders to develop and grow."

"I can see why you couldn't do all that with the amygdala pulling your strings," I reflected, thinking about what QT had done for me so far, both at work and with Grace.

I remembered something Joseph had told me in one of our early meetings: "Each time we are hijacked by the amygdala, we end up wasting time and energy that could have gone toward constructive and satisfying solutions." Wasn't this the essence of what Joseph called a Judger hijack? I wondered if Joseph was a friend of the author. Maybe Joseph himself was the author of the article, writing under a pseudonym.

I looked up from my reading. Joseph took another sip from his cup, set it back on its saucer, and looked across the table at me expectantly.

"I'm beginning to put it together," I said. "Could it be that this work of yours is reconfiguring my brain? That's the way it feels sometimes." Though I was making a joke, I must admit that his work really had given me a very different way of thinking. My brain was making vast new connections.

Joseph nodded slowly and smiled, the corners of his eyes crinkling the way they always do when he is pleased. "When I began this work," he said, "I was interested in what it would take for people to get better at managing their inner states. I knew that at the root of our Judger reactions we usually find some kind of fear, even if it doesn't look that way. Fear naturally pushes us toward Judger.

Remember that tendency of the amygdala we talked about, how when we feel under pressure or in any way threatened, our survival instincts focus on worst case scenarios, so we feel ready for whatever life throws at us."

"That's why you say we're all recovering Judgers," I interjected.

"Yes, yes! That's exactly right. Leaders need to be self-possessed—to have the awareness and skills for self-management regardless of what's going on around them, and within them. They need to be able to lead themselves before they can be truly effective at leading others. That's a good description of the process you went through in the car after we spoke that day. You literally changed your internal state, and from there your perceptions and options broadened considerably. That's what made such a difference in the conversation you had with Charles later that day.

"It's very clear that if leaders allow circumstances and feelings to take them over, they lose their ability to communicate well or be strategic and proactive. They run the risk of leading with 'ready-fire-aim' behaviors instead of 'ready-aim-fire' ones. They eventually lose the confidence, trust, and loyalty of those around them... and that's also when the collaborative spirit of a team or an organization starts to break down."

"Which is why asking Switching questions and getting back to Learner mindset is so important," I mused, thinking that this is important for everybody, not just for leaders. I drifted off for a second, remembering what Switching questions and the Learner mindset had done for my relationship with Grace. I wanted to share this with Joseph, but he was glancing at his watch and telling me about an appointment he had to keep. He stood up, reached across the table, and shook hands with me, his grip firm and warm.

There was something in that moment of contact that made me realize how much working with him had changed my life… and how I'd nearly passed up that opportunity when Alexa first told me about him. I felt embarrassed as I remembered how I'd scoffed at that big question mark on Joseph's card. My whole identity had been tied up with being the Answer Man! Today a question mark means something very different for me: it's a symbol that has become filled with possibilities…

With a number of successes behind me, I believed I had made my mark at QTec. But I was also aware of new challenges on the horizon. Alexa was developing plans for QTec's further expansion, which was making me nervous. I was happy in my present position and gaining confidence in my leadership skills. With everything going so well, I didn't want things to change. But every day I heard rumors about Alexa's restructuring of the company. This wasn't news to me, of course. But whenever I'd heard about a company restructuring it usually meant downsizing and people losing their once safe jobs.

Alexa hadn't talked to me about specific roles I might play in the plans that were underway. Would she include me in a larger leadership position? Or had my failures before Joseph's coaching given her second thoughts about me? My shoulders tensed up whenever these questions popped into my mind, signaling me that I was slipping into Judger. I tried to at least stay neutral until I could be surer of the facts.

Then one day, while I was immersed in some reports Charles

and I had been working on, the phone rang, jolting me to attention. Alexa's secretary was calling. Was I free to come down to a meeting with the boss in a half-hour or so? And would I please bring that green folder along. I'd know the one. Yes, I knew the one alright. It was the folder with that resignation letter I'd written. What did Alexa want with that? Hadn't we gotten past that business?

I finished the task I was working on, grabbed the green folder from my desk drawer, and quickly glanced inside. My resignation letter stared back at me. Should I review what I'd written? No! I tucked the folder under my arm and marched down the hall, feeling my belly knotting up. As I stood outside the big double doors of Alexa's office, I heard voices inside. That gave me another twinge of concern. Echoes of the amygdala! This time Joseph's words came back to me: "You have choice." Yes. I have choice. Time for my observer self to step up. I took a few deep breaths and steadied myself. "You can handle anything Alexa has in store for you if you stay in Learner," I reminded myself. I raised my hand and tapped lightly on the door.

"Come on in," Alexa called out cheerfully. She opened the door and stood just inside, greeting me with an open, friendly smile that lifted my spirits considerably. Joseph was sitting on one of the two overstuffed sofas separated by the wide coffee table in the meeting area. He stood up as I crossed the room. We exchanged greetings, and I sat down on the sofa across from him. For a second, my eyes were drawn to something on the coffee table. It appeared to be a framed picture turned face down.

"Did you bring the envelope?" Alexa asked, pointing at the green folder.

What envelope was she talking about? I lay the green folder on the coffee table and flipped it open. Only then did I remember the sealed envelope she'd handed me in that meeting when I tried to resign. It had been hidden under my resignation letter.

"This?" I asked, holding up the envelope.

Alexa nodded. "It's time to open it."

Joseph produced a small silver pen knife from his pocket, opened the blade, and held it out to me, handle first. "This must be done with appropriate decorum," he said, in an exaggeratedly ceremonious voice. I could almost imagine drum rolls.

I sliced open the envelope and read Alexa's distinctive handwriting on the note inside: "Ben in Joseph's Hall of Fame." What did this mean? And then Joseph was handing me that object I'd noticed on the coffee table moments before. I took it in my hands, admiring the beautifully finished mahogany frame as my eyes scanned the printed document under the glass. I thought it might be an article from Fortune or Forbes. But no, there was a photo of me at the top. Grace must have supplied that photo, since only she knew it was my favorite picture of me.

I looked up and caught Alexa's eye. "When I hired you, Ben," she said, "I knew it was a gamble since you'd never held any kind of leadership position. This was a big unknown. On the other hand, I'd also never seen you back away from a challenge, no matter how big."

"Well, there's always a first time," I said. "Had you not referred me to Joseph, I might have vanished down the highway like the proverbial Road Runner in a whirlwind of dust!"

Alexa laughed. "I doubt that very much. That's just not the way I think of you at all, Ben."

"Nobody's denying that you fumbled," Joseph added. "What impressed me was how you picked yourself up, got your hands on the ball again, and made the run for the winning score."

"Your recovery confirmed my instincts about you," Alexa said. "You see, I subscribe to the belief that failure is often crucial for learning. I was quite certain that with Joseph's coaching, you would come out on top."

Failure is often crucial for learning.

She paused, giving me time to look over the document. It was like those other write-ups I'd seen in Joseph's Question Thinking Hall of Fame, describing how different people had used QT to surmount difficult challenges. Mine described how I'd led my team to the breakthrough that helped turn QTec around. Reading it made it clearer to me how Question Thinking had helped me develop my own natural leadership abilities. Not to mention what it had done for my relationship with Grace, I thought with a smile.

As I became more confident with employing Question Thinking, I'd been pleasantly surprised to see how others around me picked up on it, almost as if by osmosis. Of course, Charles and I handed out Choice Maps to everyone on our team and posted others throughout our offices. People frequently asked questions about them. Charles and I were always glad to talk about the Choice Map. Even after our explanation a person would linger at the map tracing the paths with their finger, perhaps considering ways it might apply in their own life.

As our team put the lessons of the Choice Map into action, our work environment became increasingly relaxed and open. When one of us caught ourselves getting negative, we'd usually follow up with a spontaneous, "Sorry, I guess that was pretty Judger of me." Smiles and laughter replaced the rather downcast atmosphere of earlier times. We shared what was on our minds with greater ease and were much more creative, which naturally made problem solving and collaboration far more successful.

We all began asking more questions—Learner questions. These days I smile as I observe people deep in thought, studying their Choice Maps as they work though problems or prepare for meetings. I often reflect on something Joseph once told me: "We live in the worlds our questions create." How true that is! I have learned to listen in new ways—with my Learner ears, of course—and to stay on point even when conflicts threaten, which happens less and less frequently.

Today, my Question Thinking Hall of Fame award hangs proudly behind my desk. Another copy hangs in the Hall of Fame gallery in Joseph's office. Seeing it each day reminds me of the power of Joseph's teachings and how grateful I am for the huge difference they have made in my life.

CHAPTER 14

The Inquiring Leader

"Poor leaders rarely ask questions of themselves or others.
Good leaders, on the other hand, ask many questions.
Great leaders ask the great questions."

Michael Marquardt

One morning Alexa swept into my office waving a printout of an article from the *Wall Street Journal*. She plopped it on my desk, her face lighting up with a big smile. Before I could read the article, she explained that a few weeks ago she'd been interviewed by a reporter following a keynote presentation she'd given in Washington, DC. She had nearly forgotten about it until today when they sent her a prepublication copy for her approval.

The article was titled "Inquiring Leadership: Cultivating High Levels of Engagement, Collaboration, and Innovation in the Workplace." The lead line addressed how inquiring leadership had resulted not just in turning QTec around but in producing profits beyond all expectations. My eye went to a paragraph where Alexa had highlighted my name. During the interview she had used me as an example of the kind of leader—what she calls an inquiring leader—that we were developing at QTec. Until then I'd never seen myself as any kind of a model for other people. I hardly knew what to say. Before Alexa left my office she called Joseph to share the news with him. Later that afternoon the three of us met over a bottle of Alexa's favorite wine to celebrate the occasion and toast our future.

"This article is a milestone," Joseph said, pointing to a copy he'd brought with him. "One section especially pops out at me. You say here: 'The culture of any organization is created either by design or by default, and default typically tilts toward the negative and toward Judger. For this reason, it's critically important to build an intentional Learner culture. And this can only happen through intentional Learner leadership.'"

Alexa nodded. "QT's universality—that is, how it guides clearer, more strategic thinking and communication—minimizes interpersonal challenges, which ultimately results in greater productivity."

Turning to me Alexa said, "We've had Joseph as an outside consultant focusing mostly on individual coaching and occasional QT workshops. It's time to extend the influence of QT throughout the whole company. As you've seen with your team, QT provides a shared language, with simple, highly intuitive tools and practices."

"That's true," I said. "It seems like people are always pulling out a Choice Map in the middle of a meeting and saying, 'Hey, guys, I think we're heading down the Judger path.' Or maybe, 'Susan's insight is brilliant. It puts us right back on the Learner path.'"

"That's great to hear," Alexa replied. "QT skills have certainly caught fire with individual leaders whom Joseph has been coaching. I can envision a time when everyone in the organization will be familiar with Joseph's work."

"So, what's the next step," I asked, trying to hide my impatience. "How do you see me fitting into your plan?"

Alexa took a deep breath. "I'll start by moving Charles into your position. He's been ready for quite a while."

For an instant I found myself pulled toward the Judger path. Was this a joke? Was she really moving Charles up as my replacement? Where did that leave me? Alexa's announcement triggered some negative feelings I used to have about Charles. It took a second to give my Judger mindset a rest.

"I'll want you to coach Charles through the transition," Alexa said, nodding in Joseph's direction. And then, looking me directly in the eye, she said, "As for you, Ben, I'd like you to head up the team that will bring Question Thinking throughout the whole company, stateside, internationally, and with our virtual employees. In effect, you'll become our QT ambassador."

"Me…but…" I stammered.

Alexa grinned knowingly. "Ben, you know Question Thinking backward and forward. The unique combination of your struggles and ultimate successes gives you exactly the qualifications I want for this leadership position. I want you to shift gears and think much larger than the leadership of your current team."

I took a deep breath. "I hope Joseph will be there to back me up."

Alexa laughed. "Yes, you have my guarantee of that. We're working out the details, lining up people for your team who've been particularly enthusiastic about QT. Joseph is creating QT curriculum, including a comprehensive workbook. There'll be lively, engaging e-Learning experiences based on the Choice Map.

We've already launched individual and collaborative learning online. People are sharing Learner success stories and new ways they've discovered for using the QT tools."

"That's an exciting vision," I told her. However, as I contemplated this promotion, I felt a stab of anxiety. "This is all so new to me. Are you sure I'm ready for this? Where would I even begin?"

Alexa and Joseph exchanged glances. "You can begin by telling your own story," Joseph said. "Be authentic. Leadership is as much about who you are as it is about what you do. Tell people where you started, where you are now, and what a difference QT has made for you personally, for your team, and for the whole company.

> Leadership is as much about who you are
> as it is about what you do.

"Share your struggles along with your successes. This is a great way to build trust and alliances—Learner Alliances—that motivate others to want to emulate your attitudes, skills, and results. Your effectiveness as a leader will often depend on these Learner Alliances, with trust and mutual respect based on your example, on people knowing you've been there, you've done that, and now you live it. You empower each person to think "If he can do it, so can I," a belief made all the more real as people discover that these are practical, learnable skills, not unique traits of a single individual."

"Like the QT tools you describe in the Users Guide," I said. "They've been a lifesaver for my team and me."

Alexa nodded enthusiastically. "In today's world we need to be adaptive and resilient, able to move quickly and strategically, and I believe a Learner culture equips us to deliver on that." She paused. "There's a quote by Edgar H. Schein I've always liked. How does it go? 'The only thing of real importance that leaders do is to create and manage culture.'"

"Yes," Joseph added, "There's another part of that quote that is particularly important. Schein cautions us, 'If you do not manage culture, it manages you, and you may not even be aware of the extent to which this is happening.'"

Alexa looked in my direction. "This is an important piece of your assignment," she told me. "You'll have your finger on the pulse of QTec's culture and its impact on everyone who works here. You've graduated from being the answer man, Ben. I'm offering you the leadership position of being our global QT ambassador. Your official title will be Chief Question Officer.

"In a world increasingly complex and uncertain, where we can't depend on answers from the past, our most important skill is asking the best questions of ourselves and others. I think of inquiry as the antidote to uncertainty. This is the practical skill that will characterize the most successful leaders and organizations in the future."

For the longest time, Alexa and I sat there, eye to eye. Finally I said, "I feel like the proverbial trailblazer setting off into new territory," I said.

"You're going to discover you know more than you think," Alexa said. "I'm absolutely sure of it."

"And you come equipped with a map!" Joseph grinned, pointing to the Choice Map that just happened to be on Alexa's wall, beautifully framed.

"Right," Alexa said. "You'll have all the resources you'll need. Imagine what we could accomplish if most of us were in Learner most of the time!"

She glanced over at Joseph, who nodded. Then she turned back to me: "What about it, Ben? Any questions?"

"Questions? Oh, you bet. I've got a million of them! I've become a champion of that Einstein quote you've got posted all over the place—Question everything!"

The room was silent for a moment, and then all three of us burst out laughing.

"You two are amazing," Joseph said, after we'd quieted down. "Great things are happening around here, for everybody. Creating an intentional Learner culture—what an inspiring vision! I can't help but wonder: *What can QT make possible for all of us, now and into the future?*"

The Users Guide

In the following section, you'll find the Users Guide that Joseph introduced to Ben early in the book. I've referred to chapter names where Ben applied each of the tools.

Many organizations employ this Users Guide to focus discussion groups on areas such as leadership, team collaboration, productivity, results, communication, and innovation.

Individual readers report how they flag this section of the book to have easy access to the QT tools, in preparation for a conversation or meeting at work, or with a friend or family member.

For other Change Your Question resources, I invite you to join our Learner Community (www.InquiryInstitute.com) for free color copies of the Choice Map, our blog, our *Change Your Questions Book Club,* and a variety of other materials on our growing resource list.

QT Tool 1:	Empower Your Observer
QT Tool 2:	Imprinting the Choice Map in Your Mind
QT Tool 3:	Put the Power of Questions to Work
QT Tool 4:	Distinguish Learner and Judger Mindsets and Questions
QT Tool 5:	Make Friends with Judger
QT Tool 6:	Question Assumptions
QT Tool 7:	Take Charge with Switching Questions
QT Tool 8:	Building Foundations for Learner Teams
QT Tool 9:	Create Breakthroughs with Q-Storming
QT Tool 10:	The Top 12 Questions for Success
QT Tool 11:	Coaching Self and Others
QT Tool 12:	Inquiring Leadership: Reflections on the Power of Question Thinking

• • • • • • • • • • • • • • • •

QT Tool 1: Empower Your Observer

(See Chapter 2: A Challenge Accepted)

Purpose: To expand your ability to be more present, centered, resilient, and strategic, even under pressure. The more expansive your observer capacity, the more in charge you are of your thoughts, feelings, and actions—and the less controlled you are by other people and circumstances, even when stress levels are high.

Discussion: In Chapter 2, Joseph explains that we each have this observer capacity, sometimes experienced as viewing our self as if we were an actor in our own movie. To do this, imagine yourself in a quiet place, relaxed and comfortable. You see yourself from a vantage point of curiosity and reflective detachment, simply noticing what is. From this vantage point you may notice yourself becoming increasingly "mindful" of the role your opinions and assumptions play in your experience of the world. You will find yourself making more conscious and effective choices.

Switching into observer mode, to any degree, is an invaluable skill for negotiating change, making decisions, and operating effectively under pressure. From the observer self we are in an ideal position to think about thinking. We can recognize the kinds of questions we're asking and switch to Learner when we find ourselves in Judger.

Here are three simple ways to start empowering your observer capacity.

Practice 1: The next time your phone rings, do nothing. Just listen to the sound of the ringing, observing your reactions, such as wondering who might be calling, or the urgency of your desire to answer or check the caller ID. Just observe your thoughts and feelings, letting them go instead of acting upon them. To help you stay in observer, focus your attention on the quality of the sound of the phone as if this were the most important job of the moment. The goal here is to become more conscious and aware of the observer experience.

Practice 2: When you get into a challenging situation, step into observer mode instead of following your impulse to act or to otherwise express your thoughts and feelings. Remind yourself that, just as with the ringing phone, you do not have to "answer." Just watch and listen from your observer vantage point; you'll soon find that new possibilities open up to you. When you do take action, you will be more thoughtful, strategic, and mindful. And you'll reap better results!

Practice 3: The next time you're hijacked by Judger, take a few quiet moments to pause. Sit quietly. Remind yourself this is not the time to take action. Instead, note whatever you are thinking, feeling, or wanting at that moment. Be your best observer self, respecting this moment as an important and significant practice, strengthening your observer capacity, even if it feels like you are doing nothing.

Activate your observer self at any time by calmly asking yourself, *What's present now?* This is the quickest route to recognizing when you're in Judger and accepting that this is momentarily just the way it is. This moment of "waking up," of noting where we are, grants us the truly liberating power of choice.

• • • • • • • • • • • • • •

QT Tool 2: Imprinting the Choice Map in Your Mind

(See Chapter 3: The Choice Map)

Purpose: It's often said that while we have little control of the events and people around us, we do have choice about how we respond to them. When we familiarize ourselves with the Choice Map and imprint it in our minds, we maximize our ability to reap its rewards for choosing how we respond.

Back in the chapter titled Kitchen Talk, Ben's wife Grace grabbed the Choice Map he had placed on the refrigerator door, then raced off to work with it, having a particular need for it in resolving difficulties with a coworker. This scene captures the essence of the Choice Map as a practical tool for asking the questions and choosing the mindsets that can best guide our actions and experiences at home, at work, and in our leisure time.

Discussion: Throughout Ben's story, Joseph coaches him in using the Choice Map to look at the mindsets his questions reveal, and to recognize the results those mindsets are likely to produce. In each coaching session, the Choice Map is the key for revealing how Ben might change his questions for the best results. Here are four ways you can accomplish this:

Practice 1: Start with focusing on the image of the Choice Map itself until you imagine it in your mind's eye. While referencing this mental image, picture yourself at the crossroads on the left side of the Choice Map where some thought, feeling, or circumstance is impacting you. It might be related to your business, career, or personal life. Now start experimenting with each path—Judger and Learner—by asking yourself both Judger and Learner questions about the situation you have in mind. Take your time to consider the results each set of questions might produce. How does each path affect you emotionally? How does each one influence your thoughts and your moods? How does each one impact your actions? If you land in Judger, what Switching question might allow you to step onto the Switching Lane and return to Learner territory? Referencing the mental image you have of the Choice Map, simply ask Where am I right now? Am I in Judger? Where do I want to be? What is my ultimate goal in this situation?

Practice 2: Use your mental image of the Choice Map to learn from a past situation that did not work out well for you. Did a Judger hijack block your success? How would you handle that same situation now, using your Learner mindset?

Practice 3: Use your mental image of the Choice Map to learn from a situation that did work out well for you. What Learner questions made the difference? If Judger was present, what Switching questions did you use to avoid the Judger Pit and move onto the Learner path? What lessons do you draw from these observations that might benefit you in the future?

Practice 4: There's an old medical school saying: "See one, do one, teach one, and it's yours!" Share the Choice Map with others at work and at home. This is an ideal way to reinforce Learner relationships with people anywhere in your life. Caution: Make sure you're in Learner when you share the Choice Map with others!

(Note: Free color downloads of the Choice Map are available at my website: www. InquiryInstitute.com.

● ● ● ● ● ● ● ● ● ● ● ● ● ● ● ●

QT Tool 3: Put the Power of Questions to Work

(See Chapter 2: A Challenge Accepted)

This tool has two parts: The first (A: Internal Questions) has to do with becoming more aware and effective at asking the questions we ask ourselves; the second (B: Interpersonal Questions) has to do with becoming more prolific and effective at asking questions of others.

A: Internal Questions

Purpose: To become more aware of your internal questions, the ones you think with, and to increase the quantity and quality of these questions. Remember that asking questions and listening are two sides of the same coin.

Discussion: Ben starts to change when he realizes that the questions he asks himself—both Learner and Judger—impact the results he's able to achieve. He then begins refining his questions by applying the tools in the Question Thinking system.

Our actions are driven by internal questions that we may or may not be aware of asking ourselves. Some may even marinate for years before we become aware of them. Even an ordinary activity such as getting ready to go on a family vacation is driven by questions. For example, when packing for a trip, you went to your closet, your bureau, and your medicine cabinet, asking yourself questions such as: What climate(s) will we be in? Do I need evening as well as casual clothes? What packs well and doesn't wrinkle? And, How long will we be gone? You answered your questions first in your mind by making a choice, followed by doing something such as placing certain items in your suitcase.

You would ask yourself very different questions depending on your destination, say, an African safari versus a lovely week in Paris. And what if you arrived at your destination and discovered you'd forgotten something? That just means you forgot to ask yourself about that item when you were packing.

These two practices for increasing your awareness of internal questions, or Self-Q's, are very simple. The first turns your attention to how prevalent internal questions are in your life. The second focuses on the types of questions you typically ask yourself and the kinds of experiences and results they produce.

Practice 1: When you get up tomorrow morning, do a little personal question research. Note the questions you're asking yourself as you get dressed. Then, from time to time throughout the day, ask yourself what questions might be driving your behavior in the situation, both in terms of your own actions and interactions with others. It takes patient observation to recognize those behavior-generating questions, but if you stay with it you'll see the influential role internal questions play in your life.

Practice 2: As a second piece of internal question research, notice your responses to situations that come up throughout the day. Is your first thought a statement (an answer), or is it a question? If your first thought is a statement, change it into a question; notice how shifting from a statement to a question changes your mood, actions, or interactions. Notice any correlations between your statements or questions and the kinds of experiences and results they produce.

Practice 3: To be a great listener, first pay attention to what you are thinking. Then put those thoughts aside so you can hear the other person. It's difficult to hear what others are saying if you are only listening to yourself. Listen with Learner ears rather than Judger ears.

B: Interpersonal Questions

Purpose: To become more aware of the questions you ask other people, including their impact on them, and to affect the quantity, quality, and intention of your interpersonal questions.

Discussion: Throughout Ben's story, Joseph helps him to understand the importance of asking questions in order to:

- Gather information

- Create understanding and learning

- Build, improve, and sustain relationships

- Clarify and confirm listening

- Stimulate creativity and innovation

- Resolve conflicts and create collaboration

- Search for and challenge assumptions

- Set goals and create action plans

- Explore, discover, and create new possibilities

Practice 1: Approximately what is the ratio of questions you ask to statements you make (your ask/tell ratio)? Do you tell more than ask? Practice asking more questions and telling or advising less. What do you notice when you do this?

Practice 2: Recall a time when a particular question made a positive difference in your personal or professional life. What was the question? What was the result? And what was it about the question that made such a difference?

● ● ● ● ● ● ● ● ● ● ● ● ● ● ●

QT Tool 4: Distinguish Learner and Judger Mindsets and Questions

(See Chapter 3: The Choice Map, for the list of Learner and Judger Questions)

(See Chapter 6: Switching Questions for the full Learner/Judger Chart)

Purpose: To distinguish between our Learner and Judger mindsets and notice how each affects our thinking, feeling, actions, relationships, and results.

Discussion: In Chapter 3, Ben uses Joseph's list of Learner/Judger Questions to identify the kinds of questions he's asking and their effect on him, other people, and specific situations. As he gains greater facility with Question Thinking, Joseph introduces tools to identify Learner and Judger mindsets and relationships.

The following exercise allows you to experience what Ben experienced as he refined his ability to recognize intellectual, emotional, and physiological differences between being in Learner and being in Judger.

Practice: Look at the Judger column of the Learner/Judger Questions and notice how the questions affect you physically, emotionally, and intellectually. If you're like most people, Judger questions may cause you to feel deenergized, fearful, negative, tense, or even a little "blue." In QT workshops some people report that they held their breath or got a headache from thinking with Judger questions!

Now switch to Learner. Take a deep breath, let go of Judger, and slowly read the Learner questions on the right side of the chart. Notice how you feel now. Many people report that Learner questions make them feel energized, optimistic, open, hopeful, and more relaxed. They feel encouraged to look for solutions and possibilities. As one man noted, "When I'm looking with Learner eyes, I feel hopeful about the future."

Most people report that the questions associated with these two mindsets put them in distinctly different moods—positioning them to think, feel, act, and behave accordingly. In what ways do Learner and Judger mindsets affect the world of experience and possibility for you?

Explore how one or the other mindset influences your interactions with other people. How does Judger mindset—yours or theirs—affect communications and connections with others? Switch to Learner mindset and note how this affects your interactions with others. Then ask yourself about the impact of Learner mindset in similar situations.

● ● ● ● ● ● ● ● ● ● ● ● ● ● ● ●

QT Tool 5: Make Friends with Judger

(See Chapter 4: We're All Recovering Judgers)

Purpose: Being more aware and accepting of Judger mindset in ourselves and others.

Discussion: As Ben grows increasingly aware of his Judger (Chapter 4), he discovers that he often becomes the target of his own Judger mindset. Joseph coaches him through this seeming double bind by encouraging him to make friends with Judger.

Although it may seem counterintuitive, the more accepting we are of Judger, in ourselves and others, the stronger is our ability to switch to Learner where we are most resilient, centered, resourceful, strategic, and better able to connect with others.

Practice 1: Consider keeping a small journal to make brief notes when you observe yourself and others in Judger. Include Judger questions you notice yourself asking as well as any physical sensations or moods you associate with Judger. This builds awareness of Judger.

Practice 2: Place a rubber band around your wrist and lightly snap it whenever you notice you've been hijacked by Judger, simultaneously congratulating yourself for your increased awareness of Judger!

Practice 3: Give yourself a 10-minute period in some neutral situation, such as watching TV, to be deliberately Judger. For example, be openly judgmental of a newscaster's hair style, voice, or clothing. Note your feelings and thoughts as you do this. Your easy familiarity with Judger heightens your ability to switch to Learner.

Practice 4: Be careful not to go Judger on Judger! Whenever you recognize you are being judgmental about your own Judger, or someone else's, step back and congratulate your observer self for doing its job. Through this awareness you gain the freedom to operate from Learner and position yourself for better results.

• • • • • • • • • • • • • • •

QT Tool 6: Question Assumptions

(See Chapter 10: When the Magic Works)

Purpose: To minimize mistakes and suffering from unintended consequences based on false, unvalidated, or incomplete information.

Discussion: In Ben's story, both he and Grace make faulty assumptions that undermine effective communication and creative thinking. Faulty assumptions can sabotage our efforts to achieve our goals and deepest desires, including our ability to build and maintain satisfying relationships. As they bring blind spots in their assumptions to light, Ben and Grace expand their options for building a more positive and satisfying future together.

How do you assess the accuracy of your own assumptions—thus avoiding your committing assumacide? Start with the courage and willingness to notice and examine your assumptions. The habit of asking skillful questions, both of ourselves and others, plants the seeds for the growth of valuable new perspectives. Asking questions to discover and challenge assumptions is essential for avoiding trouble and getting the results you desire.

Practice: Recall a situation in which you felt stuck or you wanted different results. Use the following list of assumption-busting questions to shine a light on false or faulty assumptions. Consider writing down your responses.

- What assumptions am I making about myself?

- What assumptions am I making about others?

- What am I assuming from the past that may not be true now?

- What am I assuming about available resources?

- What am I assuming about what's impossible—or what is possible?

• • • • • • • • • • • • • • • •

QT Tool 7: Take Charge with Switching Questions

Purpose: To facilitate course corrections from the Judger path onto the Learner path. (Be sure to reference the Switching Lane in your mental image of the Choice Map.)

Discussion: In Chapter 6, Switching Questions, Joseph introduces Ben to the Switching Lane—a shortcut from Judger to Learner. Think of Switching questions as turnaround or course-correction questions. They can literally rescue you from Judger experiences, giving you the opportunity not only to choose a new course but to sometimes make major breakthroughs.

By their very nature, Switching questions are *from-to* questions, meaning they can carry us *from* Judger *to* Learner. We all use Switching questions whether we realize it or not; the more aware we are of using them, the more we are able to choose them at will.

The best Switching questions are those that feel most natural to you. The following list of Switching questions includes some contributed by workshop participants.

• Am I in Judger? (This awareness is always first.)

• Is this what I want to be feeling?

• Is this what I want to be doing?

• Where would I rather be?

• How can I get there?

- Is this working?

- What are the facts?

- How else can I think about this?

- What assumptions am I making?

- What is the other person thinking, feeling, and wanting?

- What humor can I find in this situation?

- What's my choice or decision right now?

- Am I being the person/leader/parent/ etc., that I want to be?

Practice 1: Think of a past situation that was difficult or frustrating but that you managed to turn around. Try to recall Switching questions you might have used in that situation and explore why they made a difference. When you discover the questions you asked intuitively, you'll be able to use them more intentionally, skillfully, and successfully.

Practice 2: In Chapter 8, See with New Eyes, Hear with New Ears, Joseph introduces Ben to the ABCD Choice Process). Pick a current challenging situation that you wish to improve and follow the ABCD format described in Ben's story.

● ● ● ● ● ● ● ● ● ● ● ● ● ● ●

QT Tool 8: Building Foundations
for Learner Teams

(See Chapter 9: Learner Teams and Judger Teams)

(See Chapter 11: Q-Storming to the Rescue)

Purpose: To explore the benefits of applying Question Thinking and the Learner/Judger distinctions for building top performing teams and organizations.

Discussion: In Chapter 9, Joseph uses the Choice Map to explore the distinctions between Learner teams and Judger teams. Ben considers ways of turning his Judger team into a team guided by Learner principles and practices.

The experience of working on teams can be challenging, and it's all too easy to slip into Judger ways—by stopping listening, pushing one's own agenda, or blaming others when things don't work out. Participants might also go Judger on *themselves* by assuming that they have nothing of value to contribute, by shutting down or not fully engaging. Or they could go Judger on others by becoming demeaning or critical of other people or their ideas. When Judger prevails, nobody wins. By introducing the concepts of Learner teams, each participant can follow guidelines for suspending Judger and stepping into Learner, for a positive effect on everyone, increasing enthusiasm and productivity, and rewarding outcomes at every level.

Practice 1: Ask your colleagues if they've ever been on a Judger team. This usually produces some ironic laughter. Then ask if they've ever been on a Learner team. This usually produces genuine curiosity and open discussion about the differences in terms of personal experience, ease of collaboration, and rewards of being part of a successful team.

Practice 2: Using the Choice Map, discuss the effects of Learner and Judger mindsets. Include the concepts of Judger costs and a Judger stand-off in your conversation. Then introduce the principles of a Learner Alliance and discuss what it takes a team to create and commit to that.

Practice 3: Introduce your team to Q-Storming, Chapter 11. Then, Q-Storm with them to generate guidelines for communicating and collaborating more effectively during meetings, based on the Choice Map.

Practice 4: Notice whether Judger—yours or someone else's—is pointing to a concern or value that is worth paying attention to.

• • • • • • • • • • • • • • •

QT Tool 9: Create Breakthroughs
with Q-Storming®

(See Chapter 11: Q-Storming to the Rescue)

Purpose: To empower collaborative, creative, and strategic thinking to foster breakthroughs with more successful results.

Discussion: Ben's leadership development includes Q-Storming, which he learns from Charles in Chapter 11, and which contributes to a breakthrough for Ben and their team.

Q-Storming is most often used when breakthroughs are sought in decision making, problem solving, strategic planning, and innovation. It is a tool for moving beyond limited thinking and advancing to outside-the-box solutions and answers. While Q-Storming is akin to brainstorming, the goal of this practice is to generate as many questions as possible. The expectation is that some of the generated questions will provide desired new openings or directions. Typically, questions open thinking, whereas answers often discourage further discovery.

Q-Storming is based on three premises: (1) Great results *begin* with great questions; (2) most any problem can be solved with enough *right questions;* and (3) the questions we ask *ourselves* often provide the most fruitful openings for new thinking and possibilities.

Q-Storming is typically done with a group or team, especially when exploring new directions and possibilities. It is also used in goal-oriented conversations between two people, for example, in coaching, leadership, management, and sales. Q-Storming can be done in person or *virtually,* say, with a global team or a coaching client in a different geographic location.

The facilitator, along with the team, focuses on developing a robust goal for the session and eliciting assumptions about that goal before the question-generation phase begins. At the end, action plans are often made or revised based on discoveries made during the Q-Storming session.

Question Guidelines

- Questions should be first-person singular or plural, using "I" and "we." You want new questions to *think with,* not necessarily to ask of someone else.

- Generate questions from Learner mindset and avoid Judger.

- Questions are mostly open-ended, not closed ("How can I?" rather than "Can I?" and "How can we?" rather than "Can you?").

- Invite courageous and provocative questions, as well as "silly" and "dumb" ones. Go for quantity, not quality.

Note: Q-Storming is a powerful tool for creative thinking, so experiment with it freely. For groups or communities facing complex or challenging issues, professionally trained Q-Storming facilitators are available at: www.InquiryInstitute.com.

• • • • • • • • • • • • • • •

QT Tool 10: The Top 12 Questions for Success

(See Chapter 10: When the Magic Works)

Purpose: To provide a sequence of questions for individuals and teams to creatively think through projects and goals before introducing change and embarking on new directions.

Discussion: In Chapter 10, Ben is caught in traffic and distressed about upcoming meetings with Alexa and Charles. He calls Joseph, who gives him three of the *Top 12 Questions for Success.* These questions launch Ben's breakthroughs with Question Thinking for greater success and satisfaction, both in his work and in his relationship with his wife Grace.

The *Top 12 Questions List* can be used in at least three ways:

1. It is a logical sequence of questions to help you work through any situation you might want to change or improve.

2. You might just want to scan the list for questions you're missing.

3. You can turn to these questions whenever you're looking for just the right question to emphasize in a particular situation.

These questions are applicable for a wide variety of life's challenges. So, you'll find it useful to integrate these questions into your everyday thinking. When a challenge arises, you'll be able to naturally recall a question that can help you.

Practice: Think of a situation in which you are stuck or wanting to change. Within that situation, you can ask the questions on

the following list from several perspectives. Ask them of yourself—
What do I want? Ask them of other people—*What do you want?*
Or ask them of others with whom you have an ongoing relation-
ship—*What do we want?*
Here's the list:

1. What do I want? What are my goals?

2. What assumptions am I making?

3. What am I responsible for?

4. How else can I think about this?

5. What is the other person thinking, feeling, and wanting?

6. What am I missing or avoiding?

7. What can I learn
   —from this person or situation?
   —from this mistake or failure?
   —from this success?

8. What questions should I ask (myself and/or others)?

9. How can I turn this experience into a win-win situation?

10. What's possible?

11. What are my choices?

12. What action steps make the most sense?

Keep this list in a handy place where you can refer to it often.
Better yet, commit these questions to memory so they'll become a
natural part of your thinking.

● ● ● ● ● ● ● ● ● ● ● ● ● ● ●

QT Tool 11: Coaching Self and Others

Purpose: To spotlight special features of the usefulness of the QT methodology for coaching yourself and others.

Discussion: In leadership positions, one is often called upon to guide other people through issues and goals they've presented in their work. Notice that Joseph's methodology throughout the book focuses on helping Ben ask questions that lead him to finding resolutions; at the same time, he is teaching Ben the methodology for doing it on his own—self coaching.

This two-pronged approach facilitates a collaborative relationship between coach and client. It sends the message that while you are not there to fix the person you are coaching, or resolve their issue, that person will be learning skills, tools, and methods for resolving issues and accomplishing goals on their own. Acting as a coach, in the way Joseph did in the story, you provide a safe environment for the person you're coaching to gain practical experience with these methods. In this respect, you are equipping them for self coaching and for being more effective in whatever they do. They can even become more effective in their work with coworkers.

If you are mainly interested in QT for your coaching practice: Read Ben's story from Joseph's perspective, following how he works with Ben, using this two-pronged approach. For example, early in the first coaching session (Chapter 2) Joseph tells Ben how the QT methodology he'll be learning creates a foundation for making wiser choices, asking more and better questions, and getting better results in everything he does. As Ben's coach, Joseph makes it clear that learning the QT methodology is an integral part of the work they'll be doing together.

Joseph goes on to share with Ben some of the theory behind this work and then presents the first skill, "Tool 1: Empower Your Observer," the first tool in this Users Guide.

Near the beginning of any coaching engagement, turn the client's attention to the Choice Map, orienting both you and your client for the conversations ahead. This is also valuable with virtual sessions such as Zoom. When your client has a Choice Map in front of them, the coach can ask, "Where would you place yourself on the Choice Map right now? Are you in Judger? Are you in Learner? Are you at the Judger Pit? Are you at the Switching Lane wondering what to do next?" A quick glance at the Choice Map is instructive for both coach and coachee.

As your client's knowledge of the methodology grows, sessions become increasingly collaborative, with both you and your client applying QT for clarifying goals and resolving issues. Through this joint approach, clients become more self-aware and more skillful at self-management and self-coaching. They gain skills and confidence for building collaborative relationships with colleagues and teams beyond the coaching relationship.

Bear in mind that the Choice Map itself, being highly intuitive, tends to work as an organizing image in the brain. When fully integrated into your thinking, just recalling this image makes the simultaneous coaching/teaching elements of the methodology second nature to you and instantly available.

As you get ready to share the Choice Map with a client, consider where you would locate *yourself* on the map. If you discover you have some Judger going on, ask yourself: *What is my Judger trying to tell me? What Switching questions could help me move into Learner? In what ways could the Choice Map be most helpful to my client today?* Remember that Learner mindset is the coaching mindset.

Use these same QT methodologies to explore ways to stay in Learner throughout any conversation, whether with a client or someone in your personal and professional life.

● ● ● ● ● ● ● ● ● ● ● ● ● ● ● ●

QT Tool 12: Inquiring Leadership: Reflections on the Power of Question Thinking

(See Chapter 14: The Inquiring Leader)

Purpose: To focus on the methods, benefits, and outcomes of Question Thinking as demonstrated in Ben's development as an inquiring leader.

Discussion: In today's business and organizational life there is increasing awareness of the need for leaders who possess highly developed self-management and social skills. Daniel Goleman, author of *Emotional Intelligence,* stated that as we become focused more and more on intellectual and knowledge-based services, people skills become "ever more important, in teamwork, in cooperation, in helping people learn together how to work more effectively."

In *Fortune* magazine, David Rock further reflects: "The ability to work well with other people in a group depends on our ability to appreciate other individuals' emotions. A boss who knows what his staff members really want and care about will be able to design a better team environment than one who is simply focused on the elements of a project."

Throughout *Change Your Questions,* Alexa, Joseph, and eventually Ben represent a composite of the virtues, qualities, and characteristics of what, in this book, I call Inquiring Leadership. These abilities include being open-minded and curious as well as decisive. Inquiring Leaders are self-aware, self-reflecting, and committed to continuous development, both for themselves and for those around them. They are resilient, adaptive, creative, and comfortable with "not knowing." They think, collaborate, and lead strategically. And, of course, they intentionally ask many Learner questions of themselves and others.

Following the tenets of good coaching, covered in Tool 11, Inquiring Leaders understand that asking questions and listening make them smarter and more connected while simultaneously empowering those around them. They use Learner questions to produce powerful results both in their own thinking and decision making, and in communicating with others. They recognize the dangers and missed opportunities of not asking important questions. And they know when to stop questioning and take action!

Inquiring leaders create an intentional Learner culture where inquiry is highly valued and encouraged; they model and mandate inquiry practices throughout their organization. They *ask* more and *tell* and *advise* less, thus inviting collaboration, creative thinking, and new possibilities. Their own words, actions, and behavior invite and encourage engagement, motivation, and commitment, promoting and inspiring trust, respect, and loyalty. In Chapter 14 this is the Learner culture that Alexa, Joseph, and Ben are envisioning for the future of QTec.

As simple as it may sound, the primary goal of Ben's story is to provide a model for building self-awareness and self-management skills that are essential in today's world. Ben's development as a leader shines a light on how we become aware of our own Judger mindsets, and how Switching questions give us the power to continually reset ourselves to Learner mindset. These QT self-management skills, guided by the Choice Map, are the heartbeat of Inquiring Leadership. Using these tools leads to increased self-confidence, relaxed self-control, emotional dexterity, and the ability to be present and effectively responsive to people and circumstances. This is how inquiring leaders create Learner cultures!

With the help of the Choice Map, and inspired by Ben's story, it is my belief that the lessons of QT will prove their value in your everyday life. Look for opportunities to apply what you have discovered in this book. Remember that leaders lead by example and by empowering others. Whether or not you're in a formal leadership position, there are always areas of life where you'll be called to the challenges of leadership, be they in your family, with friends, or in virtually any social situation.

Change Your Questions, Change Your Life Discussion Guide

Because *Change Your Questions, Change Your Life* is written in the form of a modern fable—with characters representing authentic challenges, with a story drawn from real life—readers not only get clearly written instructions but a picture of the benefits when those lessons are applied. The choice to present it in this form was based on research which has shown that we best assimilate new information either through anecdotes or through witnessing it working for another person.

As you've discovered, the book teaches about mindsets and questions, and how they influence our actions, the limits of our knowledge, the effectiveness of our actions, our feelings about ourselves and others, and the results and satisfactions we find in our work and personal lives. It does this through Question Thinking (QT)—a system of practical, easily learned tools and principles invented by Joseph S. Edwards, the executive coach who leads the book's action.

Other characters—Ben, Grace, and Charles—represent people who are each working their way through job-related challenges. We read how Joseph's Question Thinking tools help them recognize and make informed choices between Judger and Learner mindsets and questions, leading to new levels of quantifiable personal and professional development.

Finally, there is Alexa Harte, the CEO of QTec, an extraordinary boss who, armed with the wisdom of Question Thinking, leads the company to success. Her genius as a leader is found in her ability to inspire her employees, building a Learner environment that brings out the best in each person.

With the above points in mind, consider and discuss the following:

1.   As the story begins, what do you notice about Ben's mindset? How do you see his mindset affecting: (a) his feelings about himself, (b) his effectiveness as a team leader, (c) his ability to work with Charles, (d) his marriage with Grace, and (e) his future as a leader?

2.   One of the first lessons of the book is found in two words that Ben first notices in a gilded frame on the wall of his office: "Question Everything!" Discuss how this simple quote—borrowed from Albert Einstein—applies to Joseph's teachings. How could asking more questions support you and others in your life?

3.   In Chapter 2, you are introduced to Grace, Ben's wife. What did you notice about their relationship, and which aspects of Ben's mindset do you feel create the greatest challenge if that relationship is to be successful? Also, discuss how the tensions in

their marriage might impact Ben's performance at work. Do you have areas in your life where your mindsets create some challenges?

4.   Turn to the Choice Map, Chapter 3, and recall a challenging situation from your own past or present. From the perspective of what you've learned about mindsets, describe what it was like to be in Judger during that experience. What Judger questions ran through your mind at that time? Then describe how the Switching Lane and asking Learner questions helped to change your mindset, your actions, or your outcome.

5.   One of the most powerful tools in your QT kit is the one about stepping into your observer self and asking Switching questions. Notice what changed in Ben and Grace's relationship in Chapter 12, *"Amour, Amour,"* when they asked different questions. Recall moments in your own life when you had a siilar experience. How might changing your questions make a difference in a present relationship?

6.   If you are working with a team or looking for a way to get through a challenging situation in your personal, professional, or community life, consider using Q-Storming, as described in Chapter 11 and in tool #9 in the Users Guide.

7.   Discuss how you, your department, your organization, family, or community might employ Question Thinking tools that lead to innovative solutions and more successful relationships.

8.   Discuss how Learner thinking might make it easier to find common grounds in social media and public dialogues.

Notes

Foreword: David Wolfskehl is the reader whose successful application of the principles of Question Thinking was described in *Inc. Magazine*. See Leigh Buchanan, "In Praise of Selflessness," *Inc. Magazine* (May 2007).

Introduction: This quote about my work is from *Coaching with the Brain in Mind: Foundations for Practice* by David Rock and Linda J. Page (John Wiley & Sons, Inc. Hoboken, NJ, 2009), 153.

Wharton@Work Newsletter of Wharton Business School at the University of Pennsylvania (August 2012), *Nano Tools for Leaders* ®"Shifting Mindsets: Questions That Lead to Results."

My textbook in cognitive-behavioral psychology, *The Art of the Question: A Guide to Short-Term Question-Centered Therapy,* was published by John Wiley & Sons in 1998 under my maiden name, Marilee Goldberg.

Chapter 2: The example of questions that drove the behavior of nomads was attributed to psychologist Mark Brown by Michael J. Gelb in *How to Think Like Leonardo da Vinci: Seven Steps to Genius Every Day* (Dell Publications, New York, 2004).

Chapter 6: This quote is from Viktor E. Frankl, *Man's Search for Meaning* (Beacon Press, Boston, 2006), 66. Originally published in Austria in 1946 as *...trotzdem ja zum Leben sagen: Ein Psychologe erlebt das Konzentrationslager* (which translates as... *In Spite of It all, Say Yes to Life: A Psychologist Experiences the Concentration Camp*). The English translation was first published by Beacon Press in 1959.

Chapter 7: This quote from Candace Pert, PhD, *Everything You Need to Know to Feel Go(o)d.* (Hay House, Inc., 2007

Chapter 9: Joseph Campbell's story of the farmer and the quote "Where you stumble, there your treasure is" comes from *An Open Life: Joseph Campbell in*

Conversation with Michael Toms, selected and edited by John M. Maher and Dennie Briggs (Perennial Library, New York, 1990).

This article describes research on the relationship between advocacy and inquiry on team performance. Frederickson L. Barbara and Marcial F. Losada, "Positive Affect and the Complex Dynamics of Human Flourishing," *American Psychologist* (October 2005), 678–86.

Chapter 10: The example about the effect on basketball teams of viewing videos of their successful moves in contrast to their mistakes is from D. Kirschenbaum, "Self-Regulation & Sport Psychology: Nurturing an Emerging Symbiosis," *Journal of Sport Psychology* (1984), 8, 26–34.

Chapter 13: The concept that that "we live in worlds our questions create" is a play on the title of the last chapter of my first book, *The Art of the Question.* That chapter is entitled "With Our Questions We Make the World."

Chapter 14: Edgar H. Schein, *Organizational Culture and Leadership* (Jossey-Bass, San Francisco, 2010).

Tool 12: Daniel Goleman, *Emotional Intelligence: Why It Can Matter More Than IQ* (Bantam Books, New York, 1995).

David Rock, "Why Organizations Fail," Fortune.com (October 23, 2013).

Glossary

Mindset: The beliefs, assumptions, expectations, and possibilities we hold about ourselves, others, and the world. Our mindset is not static and can change unconsciously from moment to moment, or, when we learn to master it, we can choose to change our mindset intentionally.

Question Thinking: How we think with questions and, when utilized intentionally, is a method of purposeful and skillful question asking that improves the quality and results of the questions we ask ourselves and others.

Learner Mindset: A mindset characterized by curiosity, flexibility, open-mindedness, and appreciation—all encoded in a set of beliefs, assumptions, expectations, and possibilities we hold about ourselves, others, and the world. Everyone has a Learner mindset.

Judger Mindset: A mindset characterized by the desire to be right, in control, safe, and certain, and it stems, in part, from our hardwiring for survival. Judger mindset is frequently critical and judgmental of both self and others—all encoded in a set of beliefs, assumptions, expectations, and possibilities we hold about ourselves, others, and the world. Everyone has a Judger mindset.

Choice Map: The self-awareness and self-coaching tool that illustrates the two mindsets we all share: Learner and Judger. It helps us locate which mindset we are in at any given moment. That enables us to map where our current mindset will likely take us, and can help us choose whether to proceed on our current path or Switch mindsets and travel a different route that will take us to the results we want.

Switching: This is the innate ability all humans possess to change their mindset and it is a skill that can be intentionally developed.

ABCD Choice Process: The QT tool that describes the process of Switching from Judger mindset to Learner mindset: becoming Aware of your mindset, taking a moment to step back and Breathe, getting Curious about yourself, and Deciding what to do next.

Learner Living: A commitment to create better experiences, relationships, and results in our daily lives so that we spend more time in Learner and decrease the frequency and impact of Judger.

Learner Listening and Judger Listening: The mindset through which we listen impacts how we interpret what we hear. Learner mindset listens with Learner questions such as, "What's valuable in what they're saying?" Judger ears listen with Judger questions such as, "What's wrong with what they're saying?" At any moment we can choose to listen with Learner ears or with Judger ears.

Acknowledgments

I am deeply grateful for all those who have supported me on my own Learner Living journey, sharing my belief in the transformative power of Question Thinking.

Thank you Hal Zina Bennett, my writing coach, editor, and thinking partner for over 20 years. Your wisdom, expertise, and kindness live in all my books and in my life. Thank you Anna Leinberger and Steve Piersanti for wise and assiduous guidance through the publishing process.

Thank you, Detta Penna, for your friendship and beautiful work in designing the interior of all my books with BK.

And many thanks to Debbie Berne, for the cover design of this, the fourth edition of *Change Your Questions.*

For the BK Publishers and staff—María Jesús Aguilo, Valerie Caldwell, Michael Crowley, Kristen Frantz, Katelyn Keating, Catherine Lengronne, Neal Maillet, David Marshall, Katie Sheehan, Jeevan Sivasubramaniam, and Johanna Vondeling.

My deep gratitude to the Inquiry Institute home team and advisors. They include Kim Aubry, partner and QT ambassador par excellence; Andrea Lipton, our Senior Director of Learning; and Lisa Kanda, our Marketing Director. Thanks also to Lina Avallone, Mark Brodsky, Lindsay Burr, Sam Cook, Christeen Era, Carmella Granado, Steve Miranda, Mary Pierce, Mary Power, Nancy Rapport, Becky Robinson, and Melissa Swire. My gratitude to the manuscript reviewers—Alan Briskin, Mary Gelinas, Jeff Kulick, Ella Mason, Daniel Siegel, and Susan Walters Schmid.

Special thanks to my community of friends, family, and colleagues—Joan Barth, Cecile Betit, Diane Chew, Janet Cho, Phil Cisneros, Roy and Anne Goldberg, David Grad, Karen Kaufman, Bev Kaye, Robert Kramer, Claire Lachance, Landmark Worldwide, Stewart Levine, Nancy Lopez, Jyoti Ma, John McAuley, Mark Miani, Ellyn Phillips, Brad Pressman, Audrey Reed, Amy Ryan Rued, Melanie Smith, Linda Noble Topf, Jessica Ventura, Gen Kelsang Wangden, Harold Weinstein, and Jim Wilson.

As always, those whom I learn from the most are my students and clients. Inquiry Institute's Chief Question Officer Certificate Program and our QT workshops bring us students who become our teachers. colleagues, and friends.

To Marshall Goldsmith who graciously wrote the Foreword to *Change Your Questions, Change Your Life*, a bow of gratitude.

I am especially blessed to travel through this life with Ed Adams, my husband and muse. He brings creativity, love, and laughter into our lives every day—although he does sometimes say, "Why do you have to ask so many questions?!"

About the Author

Dr. Marilee Adams is an award-winning author and pioneer in the fields of inquiry-based coaching, leadership, change, and organizational effectiveness. She is the founder and CEO of Inquiry Institute and the originator of the Question Thinking™ methodologies. She is also a thought leader, consultant, executive coach, and keynote speaker. Marilee has been an adjunct professor at American University's Key Executive Leadership Program in the School of Public Affairs and is an affiliate instructor for Weatherhead Executive Education at Case Western Reserve University. Marilee is a faculty member at the Institute for Life Coach Training and Expedition Coaching and is an ACC with the International Coaching Federation. She is a Fellow at the Institute for Social Innovation at Fielding Graduate University.

Marilee is the author of the internationally bestselling book *Change Your Questions, Change Your Life,* which is a #1 Amazon Bestseller in Business and Organizational Learning. She also wrote *Teaching that Changes Lives,* which brought Question Thinking and Marilee's love of inquiry into the world of education and won a Gold Medal IPPY Publishers Award. Marilee's first book, *The Art of the Question: A Guide to Short-Term Question-Centered Therapy* was lauded as a "seminal and breakthrough contribution to the field of psychotherapy." She is also the author of the *Change Your*

Questions, Change Your Life Workbook. Marilee has published articles on the expert use of questions in coaching, business, relationships, communication, and organizational transformation.

Question Thinking is known for transforming the "spirit of inquiry" into practical and powerful questioning and thinking skills and tools that make a difference in people's lives, and in organizations throughout the world. Marilee's work is considered the gold standard for excellence in inquiry in the coaching profession and is widely used for leadership, team, and organizational development.

Marilee is driven by an unrelenting passion for learning and making a difference with what she learns. She is happiest when people say things like: "Your work is so practical and it has changed my life—or my company, or my leadership, or my team, or even my marriage—Thank you!" She earned her Ph.D. in Clinical Psychology from Fielding Graduate University and her M.S.W. from Virginia Commonwealth University.

Marilee and her husband, artist, psychologist, and author Ed Adams, live in the river town and arts community of Lambertville, New Jersey. Marilee would love to hear from you at Marilee. Adams@InquiryInstitute.com.

She is available for executive coaching, keynote presentations, consulting, workshops (virtual and onsite), and coach training.

About Inquiry Institute

Our mission at the Inquiry Institute is to help create a world of new thinkers inspired by open-minded, open-hearted questioning.

Leadership, engagement, communication, collaboration, coaching, and innovation are uniquely empowered by the Question Thinking™ (QT) system of tools and practices pioneered by Dr. Marilee Adams and the Inquiry Institute. Our team of coaches, facilitators, and consultants are experts at providing QT approaches and solutions so that individuals, teams, and organizations become more successful and satisfied in realizing their desired results.

We invite you to visit our website to explore free resources, including the Choice Map, a Change Your Questions Book Club, and information about joining our active Learner Community. On the website and on the following pages you can also learn about other Learner Resources (www.InquiryInstitute.com/LearnerResources) that can make a substantial, and often life-changing difference, wherever they are applied.

Inquiry Institute:
www.InquiryInstitute.com.
Email at: Choice@InquiryInstitute.com
Phone: 800-250-7823
10 York Street, P.O Box 339
Lambertville, New Jersey 08530-3204

Learner Resources

FREE Choice Map Download: As you've learned in the book, the Choice Map is a powerful self-coaching tool to help you learn about your Learner and Judger Mindsets and discover new questions to get the results you want. To receive your free full color copy of The Choice Map, visit www.InquiryInstitute.com.

Change Your Questions, Change Your Life **Book Club:** Engage with our Learner Community by joining the *Change Your Questions, Change Your Life* Book Club! Engage with other Learners from all around the world who want to learn, engage with, and support each other with the concepts from the book. Register to join at https://inquiryinstitute.com/learner-resources.

Online Courses

The Choice Map Course: Are you curious about how you can use The Choice Map in your daily life and experience more happiness, connection, and productivity? The Choice Map Online Course will take you on the journey of exploring your mindsets and how to effectively use the Choice Map with yourself and in relationships with others. Learn more at https://InquiryInstitute.com/learner-resources.

Seven Days to Learner Living: To reinforce your Learner mindset and build Learner habits, the Seven Days to Learner Living Online Course will help you develop the strengths of Learner mindset, understand Judger mindset, and know how to Switch back to Learner when you fall into Judger. Learn more at https://InquiryInstitute.com/learner-resources.

Live Programs

Do you want Learner Living and breakthrough results for yourself, your team, and/or your organization? Visit our website Services page for details.

Question Thinking™ (QT) Foundation: The QT Foundation Workshop is a practical, experiential introduction to Question Thinking and mindset mastery. It covers the core skills, tools, and practices you need to begin your journey to more success, satisfaction, and breakthrough results.

Question Thinking™ (QT) Foundation & Practice: In this workshop you will deepen your skills with mindset mastery, Question Thinking, question asking, and communication. You will explore applications of the QT practices as they empower leaders, teams, and organizational culture. During this intensive, interactive learning experience, you will also gain new tools to bring Learner Living to every aspect of your life, both professional and personal.

Chief Question Officer® Certificate Program: This immersive training experience is for leaders, coaches, and consultants who want to embody and become expert at bringing QT practices and solutions to clients in businesses, teams, and organizations. The Chief Question Officer® Certificate Program is a transformational learning journey over six months. Upon becoming a Chief Question Officer® (CQO), you can apply to become an Authorized trainer and license the QT material for your organization and clients.

Q-Storming® Workshop: Here you learn this breakthrough process that catalyzes the discovery of new questions, possibilities, and solutions and is often more powerful than brainstorming. You will learn the foundations of the Q-Storming process that leads to collaboration, problem solving, innovation, and strategic thinking. Recommended for you, teams, project management, and organizations.

❀ Berrett–Koehler
BK̄ Publishers

Berrett-Koehler is an independent publisher dedicated to an ambitious mission: *Connecting people and ideas to create a world that works for all.*

Our publications span many formats, including print, digital, audio, and video. We also offer online resources, training, and gatherings. And we will continue expanding our products and services to advance our mission.

We believe that the solutions to the world's problems will come from all of us, working at all levels: in our society, in our organizations, and in our own lives. Our publications and resources offer pathways to creating a more just, equitable, and sustainable society. They help people make their organizations more humane, democratic, diverse, and effective (and we don't think there's any contradiction there). And they guide people in creating positive change in their own lives and aligning their personal practices with their aspirations for a better world.

And we strive to practice what we preach through what we call "The BK Way." At the core of this approach is *stewardship,* a deep sense of responsibility to administer the company for the benefit of all of our stakeholder groups, including authors, customers, employees, investors, service providers, sales partners, and the communities and environment around us. Everything we do is built around stewardship and our other core values of *quality, partnership, inclusion,* and *sustainability.*

This is why Berrett-Koehler is the first book publishing company to be both a B Corporation (a rigorous certification) and a benefit corporation (a for-profit legal status), which together require us to adhere to the highest standards for corporate, social, and environmental performance. And it is why we have instituted many pioneering practices (which you can learn about at www.bkconnection.com), including the Berrett-Koehler Constitution, the Bill of Rights and Responsibilities for BK Authors, and our unique Author Days.

We are grateful to our readers, authors, and other friends who are supporting our mission. We ask you to share with us examples of how BK publications and resources are making a difference in your lives, organizations, and communities at www.bkconnection.com/impact.

Berrett–Koehler
Publishers

Berrett-Koehler is an independent publisher dedicated to an ambitious mission: *Connecting people and ideas to create a world that works for all.*

Our publications span many formats, including print, digital, audio, and video. We also offer online resources, training, and gatherings. And we will continue expanding our products and services to advance our mission.

We believe that the solutions to the world's problems will come from all of us, working at all levels: in our society, in our organizations, and in our own lives. Our publications and resources offer pathways to creating a more just, equitable, and sustainable society. They help people make their organizations more humane, democratic, diverse, and effective (and we don't think there's any contradiction there). And they guide people in creating positive change in their own lives and aligning their personal practices with their aspirations for a better world.

And we strive to practice what we preach through what we call "The BK Way." At the core of this approach is *stewardship,* a deep sense of responsibility to administer the company for the benefit of all of our stakeholder groups, including authors, customers, employees, investors, service providers, sales partners, and the communities and environment around us. Everything we do is built around stewardship and our other core values of *quality, partnership, inclusion,* and *sustainability.*

This is why Berrett-Koehler is the first book publishing company to be both a B Corporation (a rigorous certification) and a benefit corporation (a for-profit legal status), which together require us to adhere to the highest standards for corporate, social, and environmental performance. And it is why we have instituted many pioneering practices (which you can learn about at www.bkconnection.com), including the Berrett-Koehler Constitution, the Bill of Rights and Responsibilities for BK Authors, and our unique Author Days.

We are grateful to our readers, authors, and other friends who are supporting our mission. We ask you to share with us examples of how BK publications and resources are making a difference in your lives, organizations, and communities at www.bkconnection.com/impact.